I Can't Do It...... School Is Epic !!!

Transitioning from Primary to Secondary

Rebecca Abel

Contents:

FOREWORD 6

MANY THANKS 15

ABOUT THIS SPECTACULAR BOOK 19

CHAPTER 1: MEET THE FABULOUS AUTHOR 23

CHAPTER 2: STRUGGLES AND CHALLENGES 33

    Moving school 34

    Grammar school exam 34

    Being an author 36

    Writing this book 36

    Moving House 37

    Thinking of ideas to write this book 38

    Discussing my book with others 40

    Choosing a title and charity 40

    Raising funds for this project 41

CHAPTER 3: LAST TERM IN YEAR 6 43

    School Trip/Open Evening 44

    Responsibilities 45

    Induction day 46

Time Capsule 47

Signing T-shirts/Watching video 48

Class made an iMovie video 49

Last day at primary school 51

CHAPTER 4: FIRST TERM IN YEAR 7 52

My first day at Secondary School 53

Homework 55

Behaviour at school 57

Organising yourself 57

CBBC 58

Handling money in school 60

Phones not allowed 60

My subjects 61

CHAPTER 5: WHAT PEOPLE THINK 71

Rebecca Abel's Speech 73

Asking students in primary school about their expectations . 76

Asking students who just started Year 7 in secondary school

....83

Asking students in year 8 to 11 in secondary school 96

Asking College and University students 103

3

ASKING PARENTS ABOUT THEIR EXPERIENCES IN SECONDARY SCHOOL 109

CHAPTER 6: SUMMARY OF MY PROJECT...........................128

- Nerves 131
- Friends 132
- Different types of secondary school 133
- More effort 134
- Getting involved in activities 135
- Homework 136
- Freedom/independence 136
- Age 137
- Bullying-seniority 137
- Corporal punishment 140
- Physical provision 141
- Preparation 142
- Checklist 143

APPENDICES 145

- Please fill this page if you are in primary school. 146
- Please fill this page if you have just started Year 7 in secondary school. 147

PLEASE FILL THIS PAGE IF YOU ARE IN YEAR 8 TO 11 IN SECONDARY SCHOOL 148

PLEASE FILL THIS PAGE IF YOU ARE IN COLLEGE AND UNIVERSITY. 149

PLEASE FILL THIS PAGE IF YOU ARE A PARENT/GUARDIAN. 150

FUNDRAISING 151

#SCHOOLISEPIC 152

FEEDBACK – TELL ME WHAT YOU HAVE LEARNT 153

SOLUTION 154

Foreword

"I was poised to meticulously read the book with a view to putting the narratives in structured English but, WOW, I did not know when I finished reading the last sentence in the book! I was just carried away by the literary ingenuity and excellence contained in a book written by a young author at the age of eleven years. The young author has displayed a rare skill in the fundamentals of communication by being incisive in information delivery together with logical and coherent sequence in expressing ideas and opinions on issues. Her style of writing is unique and pungent with a tincture of subtle humour. She has whetted my appetite and I have no doubt in my mind that the young author (Rebecca) is going to be a prolific writer in investigative journalism in the print and social media. There is an adage by the Yoruba people in Nigeria which says that, while watching through a window, a young child cannot get a wider view than an elder even if he or she stands on a chair. The author has just defied that adage because in this instance the elder might have been grappling with what is within the grip of the young child: that is talent or skill. In other words, the author does not need a chair but has availed herself of a ladder positioning her right on top of the elder. As the author has indicated in this book that she has flair for writing and that we should expect many more books from her in future. May the

Almighty God grant her success and fulfilment in her works in Jesus' name (Amen)".

Mr Emmanuel Olabode Babatunde
(Rebecca's GrandFather)

"It's brilliant that Rebecca has shared her own experience which makes it very relatable to her readers.

I like that she has shared about what she likes as well. I know that her writing will inspire other young writers out there.

I would encourage every parent out there to buy this book for their young son or daughter who is about to start Secondary School.

Well done Rebecca. I am glad you took out time to write this. By doing this, you are helping make an impact in the world."

Phinnah Chichi Ikeji
Editor in chief
INSPIRING TEN2TEENS MAGAZINE
Communication Strategist/Tween-Teens Coach/Mentor
Author of the **Daily Affirmations for Tweens and Teens** book

"As a parent and a teacher, I have experienced so many children transition from primary into secondary school and I know it's such a big jump. So many children end up struggling if the right support is not in place. Reading through the very first chapter of Rebecca's book confirmed some of the thoughts I had.

I am so impressed at her commitment and dedication to write a book from start to finish from a child's perspective on how to help other children navigate through and manage that big jump.

I know that this book will bring answers to so many questions that might be going on in the minds of children and it will also help to prepare us parents for what lies ahead as our children move from primary to secondary school.

I know Rebecca wants to be an author and a teacher and would like her to know that she's got herself a mentor!

I fully endorse this book."

Shola Alabi
Qualified Teacher, Author, Speaker
Founder of 'Raising Successful Children Hub'
www.sholaalabi.com
www.membershub.sholaalabi.com

"The proficiency of education has an overwhelming influence on the lives of all children, from academics advancement to social empathy, eventually informing the way adults' lives being assigned.

The child-focused environment of a primary school can be hard to reproduce in a secondary school where children are expected to adjust to multiple staff, form new relationships in an unfamiliar setting and adapt to changes in routine.

Also, secondary school requires a superior level of toughness, self-organization and responsibility among pupils, therefore the process of transitioning poses significant challenges for most children.

This amazing Child Author -Rebecca Abel has graciously put together her experience during transition and a well-thought out approach of adaptation that any child going through similar process can appreciate and apply. She includes adult perspectives, experience, and survey-based evidence to back up her points.

This is a book for every child in primary school preparing to go into secondary and for parents who are concerned and looking for how to help their children overcome this new hurdle."

Dr Kenny Akindele-Akande
Author of **Finding Happiness**
Dentist, A Life Performance Coach, and Motivational Speaker

"The book entitled 'I Can't Do It Yet...But School Is Epic' and written by Rebecca Abel is a book very relevant to educational issues affecting children transiting from primary school to secondary school in contemporary times. The young author has demonstrated the ability to express herself in a creative manner that is not only appealing to her peers but to adults as well. Readers, especially children worldwide will find the book useful and educating in an entertaining manner. The author has been able to express her fears, expectations and experience while transiting to the next tier of the educational system. Parents, guardians and other stakeholders will be able to comprehend better the challenges faced by children and offer appropriate counselling and guidance. The book is recommended for children and adults, not only in Britain but in all continents of the world".

Dr Oluranti Adedayo
Chief Lecturer,
Mathematics and Statistics Dept,
Federal College of Education(T) Akoka
Nigeria

"A subject that has been overlooked for many years, is finally noticed and addressed by 11year old Rebecca Abel. With inspiration, research and hard work, Rebecca has compiled valuable information ,advice and implementation for struggling students and parents during the transitional years,6 to 7...(Primary to Secondary education).

A definite author in the making and can affirm the content of this book to be exceptionally useful.

I was delighted to discover that George Eliot and I share birthdays, plus the various refreshers on certain subjects made enjoyable reading and was clearly outlined.

Reading this book is time well spent and will help to alleviate fears, anxieties and doubts from parents and pupils, equipping confident and courageous pupils in times of uncertainty .

Well done to Rebecca, her parents and all contributors to this excellent project. This book will be a point of reference for many years to come".

Pastor Paulette Matthews
New Testament Church of God
Nuneaton

"I have had the privilege of knowing Rebecca starting as a spiritual adviser and close family friend to her parents which has endeared me as a family member to the Abels. Watching Rebecca grow from a baby to a beautiful young girl in the Lord, I have seen her transitions from nursery right up to her secondary. She has been a forerunner not only to her sisters but for many young believers in the work of the Lord and also a challenge to them in academia. Along with the traits that come with being the first child, Rebecca has shown great responsibility and passion in helping others both in their walk with the Lord and to ensure that they have a smooth transition from primary school into secondary school.

From my 25 years in the ministry, in which I have mentored children and youth spiritually, emotionally and academically, I am confident this book will be a blessing and of tremendous help. This book will not only be a benefit for students going through or about to go through the transitions but even parents who are anxious about the next stages of their child's life.

The content of this book and the amount of effort put in by the author showcases her talent and passion for writing. The content of this book without a doubt will help to answer the questions that many young children have regarding their transition from primary to secondary.

Much has been written today on the subject of transitioning from primary to secondary from the adult perspective, but Rebecca's book offers a unique view under transition for children by a child who has freshly gone through the transitioning and still adjusting to secondary school.

It is a bonus that Rebecca has collated data from freshly transitioned students, students looking forward to transitioning, and those who have transitioned in different decades. It has allowed her to pick out typical problems and solutions experienced when progressing from primary to secondary education; thereby making it more relatable.

And who better understands students on transitioning than a child who has just transitioned.

Rebecca's data collection and analysis have enabled her to give a conclusion to her readers on the transitioning process, that's far more relatable.

This book will help put to rest the fears students and parents face while they look forward to the transitioning from primary to secondary and also gives a glimpse of what to expect in their future academic pursuits."

Mrs Shade Tennyson-Kpohraror
Christian Youth and Children Mentor
Narrow Way Christian Church of God
Romford

"What a fantastic idea 💡 children writing for other children! Rebecca's writing is well organised and easy to read with its sensible approach to preparing for this next important step in life, Rebecca was clearly well prepared for secondary school and she is able to transfer her positive outlook to others.

This is not just another book of advice. With its colourful illustrations and Rebecca's typical year seven witty comments, it is a must for all students going through this transition. The nerves will disappear as you relax into this beautiful book. Enjoy"

Susan Sale
Smart-Write Tuition Services
Nuneaton

"A very educative and informative model book. Quite interesting indeed. A must read for transitional students from elementary school to high school. Whether you're a child or parent of a child on transit, you'll find this book interesting like a companion, a map, giving you direction or shaping your bearing, it's also like a mirror reflecting images of different people (Learners-at different times, ages, schools... But with one common ground, "Transition from primary school to secondary school")".

Rebecca Abel's 'Transitioning to secondary school' is evidently the product of a young gifted writer specially endowed to impact students on transit. The book is so absorbing that you scarcely want to put it down once you start to read. Didactic to be endorsed for readers.

Dr Olabisi Killian

Adj. Lecturer Guidance and Counselling Dept.
Lead City University
Adj. Lecturer School of Health Information Management
University College Hospital, Ibadan, Nigeria

Many thanks

So many people have helped me to achieve this dream of being an author but firstly I'll like to thank **God** for making it happen. Secondly, I want to thank my family for supporting me. My Mum and Dad supported me greatly especially my mum who extremely motivated me to produce this book. Here is a list of people who supported me financially, spiritually and physically:

- Pastor Paulette Matthews, Dr Felix Ikie, Mrs Oluwatobi Olure, Mrs Victoria Adeseye, Mrs Oyegunle, Mrs Nora Roberts, Miss Joy Babatunde, Mrs Omowunmi Oladipo, Mrs Toyin Dennis Okunseri, Mrs Olubunmi Akinwale, Aunty Eucharia, Mrs Opeyemi Jaunty, Mrs Borokini, Mrs Adeyinka Jinadu, Dr Bisi Oke, Mrs Jackie Reynolds, Mr Deji Ogunlaja, Mrs Kehinde Jebutu, Mrs Vicki Bailey, Mrs Patricia Ojo, Mrs Shola Alabi,

Rev Ajimatanrareje, Mrs Adelekun, Mrs Susan Sale, Pastor Odunayo Ayo-Ajala, Mr Agboola Bamigbele, Dr Florence Jimoh, Mrs S. Tennyson-Kpohraror (and many more who will support me after publishing) for their donations

- Nima Thapa Magar, my very good friend for writing up most of the riddles and jokes
- Shannon Cottingham, my very good friend, for allowing me use her picture
- My form group in secondary school who voted on the book title and charity
- My proof readers - Rev. A.O.E. Abel (Dad), Dr O.K.D Abel (Mum), Mr E.O. Babatunde (Grandpa), Mrs S. Tennyson-Kpohraror, Mrs Olure
- My design feedback by Mrs Jackie Reynolds, Mrs Vicki Bailey, Mrs Amandeep Phul, Dr Kenny Akindele-Akande, Mr Anuoluwapo Akande
- Amazon Createspace my publishing company

- Dr Kenny Akindele-Akande, Mrs Shola Alabi, Mrs Tonye Adenusi, Mrs Sabine Adeyinka, Mrs Phinnah Ikeji who gave me mentoring and consultation advice
- Jacqueline Wilson a famous author for inspiring me
- Jeff Kinney a famous author for the inspiration too
- My Form Tutor who encouraged me and gave me time to share my passion with my form
- Mrs Harrison, Mrs Brown, Mrs Walford, Mrs Edwards who were my teachers in Year 5 & 6 at my primary school encouraged and taught me really well
- The Head of Year - Mrs Bagshaw – who also chose me for the speech I gave in school
- My Headteacher in my secondary school who chose and motivated me for a speech in school
- Students in my primary school who answered some questions on their feelings about secondary school

- Friends and family who answered my many questions
- My best friend Eve from my old school who also inspired me to be an author when I was younger
- My former Headteachers in my old schools who gave me awards for my writing skills like Mrs Wallis, Mrs Staino, Mrs Kaminski-Gaze
- People (like you) who are reading this book because you bought it
- Inspiration from various books I've read and to myself who thought of this idea of becoming an author
- Parents who allowed my friends to answer these questions quickly and on time

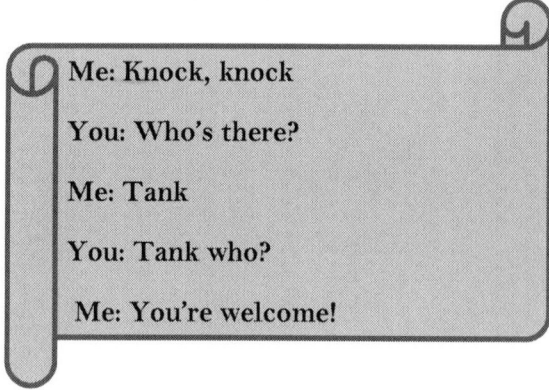

Me: Knock, knock

You: Who's there?

Me: Tank

You: Tank who?

Me: You're welcome!

18

About this spectacular book

I am sure you'll be asking yourself right now why I decided to write this book. Someone could say you can read about almost everything you need to know online. I agree, but with my experience of my transitioning process, you get a child's point of view of how things are in reality. If you read about it online, you will only get adults' (like teachers' or parents') opinion about how children feel and what to expect. Theirs is more of what an adult will want to read. ☹*BORING!* ☹ But this book links with younger children my age. Different schools have their ways of preparing pupils in primary school for secondary school by organising induction and open days, introducing the buddy system where an older student is attached to a new student, separating the new students' classrooms and play area.

However, in this book, I will tell you about the struggles and challenges students face while moving from primary to secondary. This book helps parents and

19

children to have an understanding of what to prepare for, the sudden change they may experience and how they need to grow up quickly to take more responsibility for their learning. In addition, I will be sharing my experiences of my 11+ exams to go to a grammar school, open evenings, making friends, managing workload and homework, coping with a new 'weird' environment. You know what I mean! I would love parents to read this book to discuss with their children and for children preparing for secondary school to read this book to know what to plan for.

Another beautiful thing about this book is that you will be able to read and compare questions and answers from different students' point of view at different stages of their education.

Parents are very busy with work and other things these days (like TV, phones, Xboxes and tablets ☺) that they don't give enough time to their children especially preparing them for the next stage of their lives. Some children have different homes ("suitcase kids" as described by Jacqueline Wilson) which could be a challenge to settling down. This book will show how parents think about secondary school transition from their experience in their days but it may or may not be relevant to a child in the 21st century. At the end of every chapter, there is a riddle or joke and the answers are on the feedback page (last page).

Chapter 1 is about myself and so, if you want to know more about me, read it.

Chapter 2 is about my struggles and challenges while I was preparing for secondary school.

Chapter 3 is about my last experiences in year 6 and what made me excited and nervous at the same time.

Chapter 4 is about my first term in year 7 in a new environment, how I felt and overcame the feelings.

Chapter 5 is a very exciting chapter where you get to read responses to the questions of different people from different generations, race, continents and environment.

Chapter 6 is my opinion on the responses and it shows how different people say the same thing in different ways and experience the same thing in different ways.

The reason I am writing this book is to help pupils who are nervous, unsettled or having mixed feelings about moving into secondary/high school to be more confident, aim to be the best and give them some important information they may not get from anyone else. I need to get this book into the hands of those children who will desperately need this book in the next chapter of their lives. Let's do this together!!!

Chapter 1: Meet the fabulous Author

Hi, my name is Rebecca. I am going to tell you a bit about myself. For starters, I'm 11 years old and I'm going to tell you about my transition process (moving from year 6 – year 7) @ 11 years old. I have three younger sisters called Rachel, Ruth and Rhoda. I know! If you've noticed, I have three sisters whose names start with the letter 'R' and we're all 2 years apart! I am the first-born, Rachel is the second born, Ruth is the third born and Rhoda is the fourth born.

Okay! So, my ambition in life has always been to be an author and a teacher. My friend in my old school (St Catherine's C of E Primary School) called Eve was my old best friend and we used to write stories with each other. We gave each other the stories to complete at each of our houses and when we completed it, we'd show it in assembly. So, most of my certificates have been about good writing. I have been writing ever since Reception (Nursery) at the age of five. My dream has always been to be an author. I've been to about four schools (Downfield School, Squirrels Day Nursery, St

Catherine's School, All Saints C of E School) and I'm in my fifth school right now.

Now I'm going to tell you about my favourites.

Favourite author: Jacqueline Wilson because I've read 19/50 of her books (at least) that are really good. However, I am going to read much more because I love Jacqueline Wilson books. Why? I love the way that Jacqueline Wilson writes in first person all the time. I assume that Jacqueline finds it easier to write in first person and I do too. The way of expressing her stories, style of writing and the amount of pages she writes in her book is wonderful. She has really big books - that means a lot of pages. Her recent book 'Wave Me Goodbye' was *magnifique*, (magnificent) it had 400 plus pages filled with so much detail you felt... well I felt that I was one of the characters in the book. Once you read her books, you can never stop reading them because it is as if you are one of the characters in the book. Look, I said it *again*! Jacqueline just puts vivid images in your imagination that's another reason why I love Jacqueline

Wilson books; she doesn't even use many pictures just a picture for each chapter and yet, she still puts *vivid images* in your head. I have also read 9/20 books (at least) by Jeff Kinney. Jeff Kinney writes 'Diary of a Wimpy Kid' and I find that interesting because a boy called Greg writes about his life. 'Diary of a Wimpy Kid' is a bit like 'Dork Diaries' by Rachel Rheine Russel. 'Dork Diaries' is about a *girl* who writes about her life but mostly talks about this boy in her school; also about the troubles she has with her *annoying* sister. I *have* read some Alex. T. Smith books which I find incredible; Claude is the main character in his books. I find Claude interesting because he goes on different adventures when his owners are not at home. He always has something from his adventure, his owners always ask themselves how he would have got the special object and they always say, 'he's only a dog he's been here all day.'

Favourite riddle and joke: I have two favourite riddles and a joke. The answers are on the last page at the back of this book:

1) There is a woman living in a bungalow, her sofas are purple, her bed is purple, her curtains are purple, her *hair* is purple everything in the house is purple. Question: 'What colour are her stairs?'

2) A green man lives in a green house, an orange woman lives in an orange house, a blue man lives in a blue house. Question: 'Who lives in the white house?'

3) My favourite joke is…

   Person 1: Knock, Knock

   Person 2: Who's there?

   Person 1: Doctor

   Person 2: Doctor who?

   You need to find the answers on the feedback page (Page 153).

Favourite colour: Purple is my colour and I have purple things all around my room. Light purple, violet and dark purple. I like and love purple because it makes me so happy. First, my favourite colour was pink then blue then red then purple. I think that purple is in the middle of pink and blue.

Favourite hobby: You must have noticed from my picture page that I love *selfies* especially when I have a new hairstyle! Well, I do have many things I like to do. Apart from visiting interesting places/countries, I like running (sprinting), tennis, netball, football and swimming just for fun. Well, the reason why I like running is because I have long legs (as I am constantly reminded) and I was the fastest girl in my primary school. I like tennis because I like the way you hit the ball with a racket. I just love using tennis rackets. Netball and football are just so cool. I don't know why but I just think so. And when I say swimming for fun, I mean swimming for fun. I started swimming since I was 5 because I wanted to be like Rebecca Adlington after she won the Olympics. I also tried gymnastics with my sister after we watched a film about Gabby Douglas. My sister, Rachel is the gymnastics expert - not me. Apart from learning to play my piano, I also have a YouTube channel that my sisters and I do while we have free time. My sister and I go to this club called Codeclub on Wednesdays where we have learnt how to program in Scratch, HTML, Python. We also have someone from IBM who comes to show us cool stuff you can do on the computer; creating your robots using RaspberryPi and making your own Wi - Fi. Our channel, GirlSparkles Abel, is where we do a variety of videos. We teach the little we know about Yoruba language, do challenges, teach memory verses, interview special people, tours around the world and many more. There is one video where we interviewed an author but sorry to disappoint you, it was not me. It is an author named Dr. Kenny. There is a part one and a part two of the interview. There will be one about me interviewing myself on YouTube. Watch out for it!!!

Favourite subject: My favourite subject is… well actually… I have no idea. My dad always says, 'You can never know your favourite subjects until year 9 or 10' but I love most of my subjects because they are all so interesting to learn. The one that I like now is Drama and English also PE.

Favourite song: I have many favourite songs. Like 'Me without You' by Toby Mac and 'You Lead' by Jamie Grace. These are not the only songs I know, it's just that I don't know all the other song names and who wrote them. Oh yeah, 'Smile' by Kirk Franklin. I actually like singing and I'm a good singer not a bad one! I listen to Premier Praise on DAB radio every day and it's awesome because they play my favourite songs there.

Anyway, now you've known about what I like, which author I like and other things I like, I am going to tell you something else.

I am writing a book on 'How did that happen?' but I haven't finished it. I decided to write this one first because of my target to complete it before the end of my first term in secondary school. I also needed to finish it before I am 12 years old. Also, after the interview with an author, I was inspired to start right away. When I started this book, I jotted some notes and ideas down so that it can help me while I'm writing the book. So, when I write down in my notepad, I use a special type of pen. It is very special, well to me it is, so I use a pen I like to call 'fluffy pen'. This ballpoint pen has a furry ball on the top that's all. Nothing special to some people but it is very special to me.

I am a Christian. A Baptist Christian and I attend a Baptist church, True Believers Baptist Church. My church invites young ones to love God and join us to serve God. We also need adult workers who are happy working with little children and teenagers. Therefore, I like my church because we worship God and do fun games like '66 seconds', sword drill, *Youngstars* Got

Talent and 'kahoot'. One of the reasons for writing this book is to raise funds for charity. My church is a charity that organises Youngstars club once a month for about 2 hours in Broxbourne and Nuneaton free of charge to children and young people like me in the two communities. The church needs a new church bus to pick up more people; money to rent the halls and snacks to give those who come. Some years, we have a church programme at the end of the year and Easter time; we sing songs, share memory verses and play games. I also love using the Superbook app and website when I am a bit free because it has so many videos and games that I like and are safe for children.

Chapter 2: Struggles and Challenges

This may be a very short chapter because I faced only very few struggles and challenges.

Moving school

Well, I have moved to four schools including nursery. I have been to five schools because I went to first nursery, second nursery, first primary, second primary and secondary school. Five schools! The main reason why I didn't want to move school was because I would worry about friends I won't have any more. How did I overcome that feeling? Well, I didn't actually need to worry about that because I made new friends. If you're moving school, don't be afraid of the new environment, be happy and look forward to the new environment. Now I've settled in, I can see that I didn't have to worry about anything.

Grammar school exam

When I was in year five, I did three mock 11+ exams so I could attend a grammar school. A grammar school is a secondary school where you have to write an exam to get into the school. It is also called a selective school because they choose those who write and pass their exams. The school *challenges* you to try to do your best and expects you to work at your best ability. I successfully passed 1 test but the other two schools I didn't reach the cut-off point. I missed out by 10 marks and it was really far from where I live so I was expected to put in more effort since I am outside the catchment area. Looking back now, I would have done better if I was very quick at answering all the questions. So, if you're preparing to do your 11plus exams, try to time yourself and be as fast as you possibly can. Pressure right? The one that I passed was a private school and it was too expensive for me to go. Even though I didn't get into the grammar school but hey I got into a good school. So if you are a person that didn't pass your grammar school exams/ 11+ exams, don't worry because you can achieve and prosper which ever school you are. If you *did* pass, congratulations and keep working hard in your grammar school so that you can make very good grades. I would advise every parent of pupils in year 5 to go ahead, register them and try an exam for a grammar school. Many people in my year 6 class missed that opportunity because I was the only one who tried the grammar school exam. Trying is always key and it helps to increase your confidence and to meet people your age.

Being an author

As I said near the beginning, I have always been writing ever since I was younger. My dream has always been to be an author. In my primary school in the last term of year 6, I was planning to finish writing a book so that I could give my book to the school for a goodbye present. But eventually, that didn't turn out very well because I didn't make a target. Sometimes I didn't even have time for myself. I do, but you know what I mean don't you? Read below and that tells you more about this point.

Writing this book

I had to leave this other book that I was planning to make because it was taking longer than I expected since I haven't had enough time to complete it. So, I had to leave that book and had to start writing this. I had to do this because I just moved from year 6 to year 7 so I thought it would be a good idea to help students who are worried to start high school. Since I'm in year 7, I have a large amount of homework. One thing I had to do was to balance out my time; half of the day I would do my school homework then the time that I had left in the day, I use it to touch some mistakes I have made in this book. I had to start writing out plans so that I could follow them because my mum advised me that having a plan and structure would guide me. I don't have to throw all my ideas on the computer while I'm typing up. So, while I'm writing this book, I look at the points that I jotted down and expand on them so that it's easier for me to write my book. My Aunty also suggested some ideas to me. It was a lot of work getting pictures and free images and we had to buy pictures online. What a surprise! Ain't ? ☺

Moving House

I really liked my old house although I love my new house more. It was very difficult to move to a new environment where my sisters and I didn't know anyone but now we are happy. I've actually never wanted to move because I had a lot of friends in my old school. The reason why we had to move was because my old house was very tight and small and since we have my mum, my dad and my 3 sisters including me, we are 6 in my family. Since we know many people and we have a large family, it will be a really tight space if someone comes over or if someone even has a sleep over, there won't be enough space. That's why we moved! ☺

Thinking of ideas to write this book

It is a bit of a challenge for me to write this book because I put a lot of effort in this book. As I have said, I have always wanted to be an author because I love writing. So the steps you have to take are hard/ easy steps because to write the book is the easy bit but to plan out what you have to write is hard. What I mean is, to plan it out, know when you are going to publish your book and launch it. On GirlSparkles Abel, when

I've actually published and launched my book, I'm going to show you my planning book and how I grouped them. I will also show you parts of my book and stuffs like that. I had to decide which order I was going to place the chapters as well. My planning helped me to stay focused on what to write and my notebook where I write what I've learnt at the end of each school day also helped me to write about what I have learnt in my subjects. When I started, I thought to myself that it was going to be incredibly easy but it turns out it wasn't. Guess who thought of this book? My mum! ☺☺☺ My mum thought of the idea of this book. Since I'm still 11 years old, I just recently left primary school and my mum thought that I could write a book so that people who are going to secondary school won't be afraid of secondary school.

The writing of this book started when my mum attended my Aunty's book launch (Finding Happiness by Dr Kenny) in London. We thought of a book I could write to solve someone's problem and help other people who need help in any particular topic. So, we brainstormed, got this idea and set a target on when to complete it. Since the one I was writing is still a long way to the finish point, we decided that the book I was planning to write in year 6 could still be done even though I'm in year 7.

Discussing my book with others

Many of my teachers and friends were asking me about my book they were putting me on the spot (in a good way though☺) so I had to be ready at all times. One of the days during an Ofsted inspection, I was introduced to a woman who was one of the Inspectors. My PSHE teacher told her about me and when she heard that I was writing a book, she was pleased. I was also happy.

Choosing a title and charity

I had so many suggestions in my head about the topic and we (my mum and I) kept brainstorming at home about the best title for the book. Luckily, my form tutor was very kind allowing me to use one of the Fridays at tutor time to explain my book to my form group where we watched the Introduction to my book on my YouTube channel called 'Introduction to my book'. At the end of watching the video, they were very helpful by filling in a questionnaire (Appendices) to choose one of the titles I suggested and they chose one more charity I could donate the profit to. Although my mum says we will need to find the money to publish the book, we are hoping God will provide. If *you* want to fill in your own questionnaire, whether you are in primary school, year 7, years 8 – 11, college/university or if you are a parent/guardian, go to the last few pages.

Raising funds for this project

Getting money to publish the book and choosing the publisher was a big task because my mum and I kept reading about publishers online, asking people from the library and authors because we needed a cheaper option. Mum sent messages on whatsapp, facebook, twitter etc to family and friends to support me on my gofundme website (www.gofundme/RebeccaAbel). So far, while I am preparing to publish my book, we have only managed to raise 25% of the target. Just so far for *now* because I don't want it to be *'fake news'* do I? I'm sure you'll guess what the answer is.

In my family, we save up our pocket money to buy what we want and I was saving up some of my money to publish my book since year 5. Unfortunately, some burglars stole the money away but that's a story my mum will *hopefully* write about later.

> You can see me in water but I never get wet. What am I?

Chapter 3: Last term in Year 6

Primary school is a brilliant place to be and it is where children from 4+ year olds to 11 year olds are taught by one teacher in each year. A main teacher teaches all the subjects which are mathematics, English, handwriting, Art, a bit of science, PE (Physical Education), RE (Religious Education) and History in a class. There are many children (about 20 - 30) in a class and sometimes there are teaching assistants that help children who need special help with their work. In primary school, there are play areas for children to play; there are breakfast and afterschool clubs too.

School Trip/Open Evening

I have been to more than 10 open evenings when I was only in year 5. The only open evening I did not attend was the one of my current school because my friends and I in year 6 went to a residential trip for 3 days. This is an absolutely fun time where you pack a suitcase with 3 days' worth of clothes and go on all sorts of adventures like night walk, climbing, abseiling, king swing (a massive swing that could fit two people) and many more. Mrs Bagshaw, this lady from my secondary school, came to my primary school most Thursdays. She was the head of year seven who had come to help us with any concerns or worries we might have had with preparing for secondary school. On the last two weeks of school she came to tell us what we were going to do on that day like where we have to go and what we were going to eat for lunch. She also told us what we should bring to our future secondary school – pencil cases, packed lunch or school dinners, money, homework books etc. - so that we are prepared for secondary school.

Responsibilities

The way that I got my responsibilities was by applying to get them. The only one I didn't have to apply for was being a House Captain! My house leader chose me. During my time in year six, I was a peer mediator - a person who helped people with any friendship problems like bullying. I was also a Prefect (not *perfect*) and a House Captain. A house captain is a person who is head of a particular group of people. We had house point groups; Love, Peace, Faith, Truth and Hope. I enjoyed my roles in school because that meant I had younger friends in Reception who are now in year 1.

I didn't just like my job, I LOVED my job 👍. I LOVED it because as a peer mediator I gained skills that I use in secondary school to make friends and to help people with issues *they* might have with *their* friends.

Induction day

Induction day was phenomenal. In addition, we had two days' worth of induction. I made many friends in those two days. On the first day, I hung around with students from my old school and talked to a girl named Rachel (from a different primary school whom I competed with in a Netball tournament) about the netball tournament and if she was going to join the netball team in secondary school. It was very awkward because I have only known her from a netball tournament and it's not like I've known her for more than a year or anything like that. On induction day, we were put into form groups. If you're asking, 'What is a form group' I will explain to you. Never fear Rebecca's here. ☺☺ A form group is a class that you stay in for the morning for about 20 mins where you get registered for the day. You know how you have classes in primary school like year 1, year 2, year 3 and others, well we have the year then a random letter and you go up a year the number will change so if I was in 7G, the next year I will be in 8G. Your number changes depending on what year you are and your letter stays the same. Happy now? ☹ -> ☺

Time Capsule

Anyway, where was I... oh yeah so when I was in my form group they told us to make a Time Capsule for homework. A Time Capsule is a box that you use to store your memorable and favourite items like a picture of your favourite hobby or your favourite chocolate wrapper. In mine, I put: Galaxy caramel chocolate wrapper; a picture of kneading bread dough; a set of instructions on how to make raisin bread; a wrist band from a theme park adventure island in south end and my local newspaper with me in it. Then I thought I could get a memory of my friends from primary school so I included my friendship letter 'R' my best friend gave me T-shirt that had everyone's name including Nursery! ☺☺ My classmates and all the other years wrote on my T-shirt. I loved the end of year 6.

Signing T-shirts/Watching video

After the T-shirts, we all went into the class and did some activities all day whilst a video of Gnomeo and Juliet was played on the screen. If you've ever heard of the story 'Romeo and Juliet', the movie we watched is meant to be like that but with a twist. It was all about envious gnomes who were always against each other. Red vs Blue. Gnomeo falls in love with Juliet but this is where the twist comes in. There is a catastrophe and the gardens are destroyed. A pile of rocks crushed Gnomeo and Juliet but they survived. It was quite an interesting animation.

Class made an iMovie video

My class made a video using iMovie to make a trailer and a movie for our leavers' assembly. My friends, K, L, E (I have use the first letter of their names) and me (Rebecca) had to work together to make this trailer and movie. The whole class also helped us because we put some pictures and videos of my whole class into our trailer and movie. L and E mostly left the work for K and me so we shuffled some things around and tried to make it perfect. The boys kept going, coming, going, coming, going, coming and you know what I'm going to say again *going and coming.* That was good guessing I wonder how you knew. All they did was go and do their 'boy stuff' and then they come back and say that we have had the tablet all to ourselves when all they have been doing was doing their 'boy stuff'. Oh yeah and to make the movie and trailer, we downloaded the app iMovie onto our tablet device then we started to make the trailer and movie. You can use this idea in your leavers assembly. My teacher downloaded both the movie and trailer onto a DVD so when we grow older we can dig out the DVD and replay it to remember our past and our school. If you are thinking, 'cool that's a good idea' then why not use this idea. You can bring this book, show your teachers this page number and do it or instead of doing a movie and trailer, you can do a little animation or I don't know but if this has given you an idea, then use this idea so you can express this book. Anyway, since K was good at editing the movie and trailer, as I said K was the one who thought of this iMovie idea, I decided to ask her to join our movie making mini group. Originally, it was E and me then we asked the teacher if we were allowed to have extra help. So E chose L then I chose K and everybody else got into little groups and helped on the paper work (making our name tags). Some were asked to find photos of us and when we were younger. I think we actually worked well with each other because we ended up finishing and editing our trailer and movie. However, K was also the person that suggested the mini group using iMovie so that's the other reason I chose her. E probably chose L because they were best mates. Best friends!

Last day at primary school

The last day of school was emotional for some people in my class because some of them cried when leaving their best friend or close friends. My teachers were emotional as well as students in my class. My teacher also said that she barely cries on the last days of year 6 students. Thinking about it know, I still miss some of my friends. I have made new friends in secondary school the only difference is that I'm not in the environment I used to be in.

> You will always find me in the past. I can be created in the present but the future can never have me. What am I?

Chapter 4: First term in Year 7

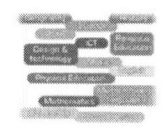

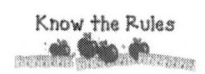

Secondary school is a bigger school with so many large rooms and big buildings with different equipment for different subjects. There are different teachers for different subjects: Mathematics, Literacy, Art, Design Technology (DT), Computing, PE, RE, Music, Keyboard lessons, Science, Drama, PSHE (Physical, Social, Health Education), History and Geography. We do DIRT (Dedicated Improvement Reflection Time) where we give feedback of our work in a lesson for each subject. We do assembly on Mondays for year 7 only and different days for different years.

My homework for PSHE was to write about my first day at school. Here is what I wrote, printed and read to the whole class:

My first day at Secondary School

Transport to school

My dad dropped me off at a reasonable distance so that I could walk to school for my first day. While I was walking to school, I felt incredibly smart. I had new shoes, my new blazer, new top and new skirt. It took me about five minutes to walk down.

In School

When I got to school, I went into the hall for assembly and I was in 7E. I felt extremely happy because I was finally in Secondary school. I am no longer in primary school. I am in secondary school. I hung around with my friends from my old school on the playground and made some new friends. My form tutor explained most of the information I needed to know; that was very helpful. What I used to fear was being bullied but I know in myself I probably won't. My priority is that, I want to be the best example somebody could ever have. The third time I went to my secondary school (after the two induction days) was awesome. Because I didn't know many people –from the first day- did not mean I was lonely. My first day of a new start was brilliant.

All of us in year 7 were given a test to write on the first day of year 7 so we could be put in classes according to our abilities. It was only year 7 students that resumed on the first day and other students joined the next day.

Some of them looked like giants and skyscrapers to me. I think that was a good idea by the school so that we could feel more confident in the new environment and so we won't be scared of the year 8s, 9s, 10s and 11s.

Homework

Most of my homework is set online on Doddle and Hegarty so you need to have a working computer and internet at home or you could use the school library (no excuse). One tip I have for you is that once you have homework, you should always try to do it on the day that you're given.

Ever since I heard about secondary school, I have been nagging my parents consistently about my new uniform. When you're in secondary, you need a reasonable sized bag to carry your homework home. You also need school money so if you want to buy food or if you've forgotten your lunch at home, you have back up food. I really wanted to wave 'goodbye' to year 6. I wanted to explore and have a new adventure. I had a big responsibility which I have been looking forward to, to pick up my sisters after school. Their school ends 3:15 while mine ends 3:00. My school is quite close to my sisters' school and I also meet my dad in the car along the way. Eventually, I got what I wanted. You also need to be responsible; grow up so that you can understand why and who you are at secondary school. When you are used to your secondary school, believe me because in 5 weeks or less, you will know your classes. My first ever school project was to make something and that something was making a dagger. Yeah! I thought so too. You must be reading my mind right now! Calm down! It's not what you think ☺ Our topic for this term is 'Tutankhamun'. Everyone should know Tutankhamun because he was an Egyptian Pharaoh! Surely you know him. This dagger was made out of cardboard; painted with wax crayon (homemade paint), yellow sugar paper and cello tape. It took me more than three days to make the dagger! My drama teacher was really pleased.

Behaviour at school

Detention rules in my school have changed. It used to be C1 where you had a warning. C2 was where you had a second warning and you would be moved to a different seat. C3 was where you had 30 minutes detention and the school will contact your parents. C4 was where you were removed from the lesson, the school will contact your parents then you would get 40 minutes detention. Harsh right? ☹ However, we now use C1, C2 and C3. I like this behaviour policy better because the troublemakers are out of the classroom in a blink of an eye.

Organising yourself

This is ... well was relevant to me. First, I noticed that my bag was always heavy. I then found out that it was because I carried all of my school books that I didn't need every day. It would be very helpful to take the books you need to school. You may have the same reason as me; the reason why I did that was because I had worry that if I forget the book at home that will lead to a detention. Look at your timetable; it will help you. Also, if you sleep early enough, you will have enough energy for school the next day. Have a bedtime even in secondary school. Always hang your uniform, keep your bag and shoes in the same place so you don't have to start looking for them in the morning.

CBBC

Newsround helps you to know and understand things around the world. You may be thinking, but BBC news tells you about the world, why Newsround? When you watch Newsround, you will understand more of the world also the current things happening around the world. It is basically safe and helpful news for children. This news only lasts for 2 – 5 minutes; it won't bore you as much as news that adults would watch. The time that I was introduced to Newsround was at the beginning of year six. Most people in my class thought that the reason why *Newsround* was called *Newsround* was because; it was about *news around* the world.

There is this programme called 'Our School' on CBBC that is all about students in year 7. Most times they interview them in partners and ask them different questions; the reporters that come to the school put cameras all around the school to show the drama and normal lessons that happen in the school. They do the show in series and seasons. It is an interesting *and* relevant programme for *students* in year 7. It also talks about trying harder because on the fourth week in year 7, I got a *student of the week* award.

On my seventh week during my half term/ break from school, I got a postcard from my RE teacher telling me that I worked extremely hard in my RE lessons. When I watched it in year 6, I wasn't learning anything from it, I just watched it as an entertainment. Since I'm in year 7, I can match up the worries and difficulties the year 7's on the TV may have and link it with my secondary school life. If you watched it, you would see that some of the scenes are relevant in secondary school.

Handling money in school

Yes, you get more pocket money in secondary school (well that depends on the family). The school introduced a machine where you put in money online or with cash in school so you can use your fingerprint to buy food from the school canteen. I think it's a good idea because some people could lose their money or just keep buying junk food or show off with a lot of money. You may also have people pranking you with money or someone stealing it. Most of my teachers say that you shouldn't have money on you because it could be very risky doing that. However, my mum says - since you can't have your money back once you put it on your money account – that I should keep some money in my school purse just in case of any emergencies.

Phones not allowed

Phones are not allowed in secondary school because people could misuse them; they could be playing games when they're supposed to be learning. They could video a teacher in class or threaten to call the police and many other *bad* things. I still see many people with their phones at break and lunch. It's better not to copy them because if teachers spot you then your phone will be confiscated. You may need your phone after school hours to tell your parents where you are or for some other good reasons. So, you are expected to keep it at the bottom of your bag turned off or in silent mode. Your parents can reach you with any message through the school reception if it's urgent.

My subjects

Now I'm going to give you a summary of what I learnt in my subjects so far. Other subjects like Food Technology, Spanish and so on are available in school but I don't do them yet.

In **Music**, we had to do a singing audition and I was really glad that my teacher thinks I have a nice voice and invited me to join the school choir. Now there are so many things to do on Tuesdays but I'm still thinking of how to do everything —which is not possible I guess!

So for my timetable towards the end of the day, I have music, keyboard lessons, PE and then Netball after school. If you include my swimming lessons that I do outside school, now an extra music lesson, that means I'm doing 5 important subjects in a day. If you add my new music lessons, that means I'll be doing… hhhuuu.. S – E – V – E – N important lessons in a day. However, if you add my four other subjects that I do, dun… dun… dduuuunnnn. I'll be doing E – L – E – V – E – N subjects in a day including my swimming outside of school. WOW! I'm a really busy woman on Tuesdays aren't I? Actually, I'm a really busy girl on Tuesdays☺. Do you know that a pulse is a steady beat that you could sometimes tap your foot to?

In **Mathematics**, I learnt algebra, alternative and corresponding angles that look a bit like what I drew below. We learnt about Isosceles triangles, how the sum of angles in a triangle is 180 degrees and in a quadrilateral, it is 360 degrees. The angles in black are alternate angles because they are opposite. I learnt them when I was studying for 11 plus but I understand angles better now. We also do homework and practices online using hegartymaths that is very helpful. My advice is to learn all your times table in primary school so you don't have to struggle to know it in high school. Do you know that an equilateral triangle is a triangle with three equal sides?

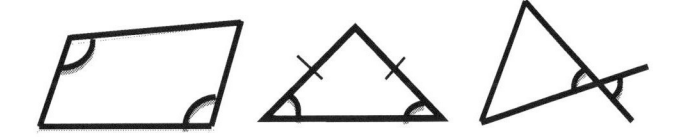

In **Literacy**, I learnt different punctuation marks which are **: ; , ! ? - ... ( )**. We also learnt about a young lady named George Eliot who was a female writer but changed her name to a male's name because of her fear of all her good books becoming a waste. Her real name was Mary Anne Evans. I have recently read some of her quotes and that has motivated me to be a female author and write. One day she wanted to be an author. Some of her quotes are:

'It is never too late to be what you might have been.'

Explanation: I think that this quote means that if you have made a tough decision in your life and you want to have a second chance, you can make things right by taking a second chance. What do you think?

'Delicious autumn! My very soul is wedded to it, and if I were a bird I would fly about the earth seeking the successive autumns.'

Explanation: I think that this quote means that if you're looking for something to achieve, you should try to find it and achieve it. What's your opinion?

'Animals are such agreeable friends – they ask no questions, they pass no criticism.'

Explanation: I think this quote means that all of us should work together to make this world a better world. Since animals all work together with no arguing or criticism like racism or being left out of certain things, we could all agree on everything and make our lives straight forward or not allow our differences seperarate us. What is your own idea?

Do you know that George Eliot was born on 22nd November 1819 in Nuneaton?

In **Art**, I sketched a cube and a cylinder. I applied tones, texture and you can shade in then smug it with your fingers to give it an effect. The feedback I got from my teacher is to sketch lightly until you get it right. Do you know that shading is the key to make things look 3D?☺

In **Design Technology (DT)**, I learnt that hardwood is a type of wood that comes from trees that their leaves fall while softwood is a type of wood that comes from evergreen trees where their leaves don't fall off. I learnt about CAD (Computer Aided Design), CAM (Computer Aided Manufacturing) and laser cutters. I also learnt about 2D design program that gives a message to a 3D printer to print and model the object you have made. My project is to make a 3D desk tidy product and for me to persuade someone to buy my product. I used chisel and mallet to take off the excess wood in my woodwork. Do you know that there is no straight line on our faces? ☺

In **PE (Physical Education)**, there was a bleep test where you have to listen to a radio that beeps a certain amount of time and you have to run from one line to another line and back. The beep gets faster and there were 10 levels. We went on to learn netball rules and a sketch of the netball court. Do you know that in netball, you can only land on one foot (landing foot) and you cannot move until the ball is out of your hands? ☺

In **RE (Religious Education)**, we are learning about the founders of different religions, how everybody is equal even though they may have a different religion to you and to respect each other. We learnt that Jesus Christ is the leader of Christians and Prophet Muhammad is the leader of Muslims. Other religious leaders are Guru Nanak (Sikhism), Siddhartha (Buddhism), Abraham (Judaism) and many more. Do you know that Diwali is a Hindu festival to celebrate a new year?

In **Computing (ICT)**, I do my programming using Audacity for developing sounds effects. I had homework about making a trailer for a movie that we had to make up and I decided to make my trailer based on the blurb of this book. There are enough computers to go round in my school and enough headsets. In my trailer, I put a mother talking to her daughter about writing a book. The scene was set early in the morning when she was about to go to school. Do you know that ICT means Information and Communications Technology?

In **Science**, we learnt about the different types of chemicals and how to wear safety goggles to protect your eyes when using them. We learnt about cells and how to use microscopes to focus and make images clearer. I do science quizzes online on Doddle. Do you know that **DNA** stands for **D**eoxy **N**ucleic **A**cid and that chloro means green?

In **Drama**, we learnt about freeze frames where you act still for a play, sound scapes is where you use your mouth and body to make sounds without using any prop. We were taught to use facial expressions and actions to show the audience what you're performing. Do you know that working together in a team is key to a successful play?

In **History**, I learnt some facts that Martin Luther King tried to stop racism, and Henry the 8th had a son named Edward the 6th after marrying and killing so many wives, Tollund man was a slave who was sacrificed to a goddess located in Denmark. I have a video on GirlSparkles Abel YouTube Channel about Vikings. Vikings believed in many gods. Gladiators fought in the Coliseum. Apparently, Rome was named after a young prince called Romolous. Romans were keen on keeping themselves clean. Do you know that the Romans built most of the roads and buildings we have today?

In **Geography**, we learnt in the first week that geography is about places in the world and about maps. There are different types of maps: road maps, political maps, topographic maps and physical maps. There are 3 types of geography: Human, Physical and Environment

Geography. A way to remember North – East – South – West is **N**ever – **E**at – **S**hredded - **W**heat ☺. Do you know that there are 7 continents (Asia, Africa, Europe, North America, South America, Oceania/Australia, Antarctica) and 5 oceans (Pacific Ocean, Indian Ocean, Atlantic Ocean, Artic Ocean, Southern Ocean)?

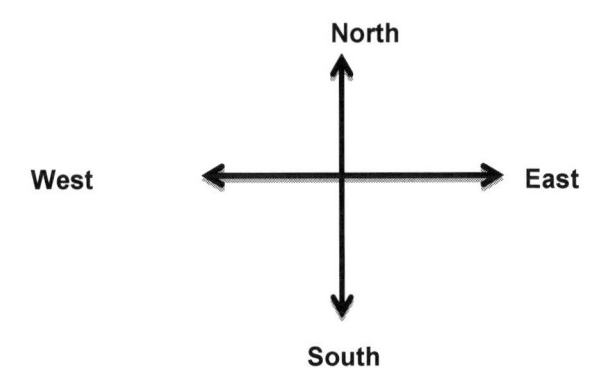

```
                    North
                      ↑
                      |
     West  ←——————————+——————————→  East
                      |
                      ↓
                    South
```

In **French**, we learnt to say and write sentences like:

How are you? – Comment ca va ?

I am fine thank you – Ca va bien merci

My name is – Je m'appelle

How are you? - Comment t'appelle tu?

I am okay – ca va comme ci comme ca

How old are you? - Quel age a tu?

Where do you live? - Ou habites tu?

When is your birthday? – C'est quand ton anniversaire?

Numbers 1 to 20 - Un, Deux, Trois, Quatre, Cinq, Six, Sept, Huit, Neuf, Dix, Onze, Douze, Treize, Quatorze, Quinze, Seize, Dix-sept, Dix-huit, Dix-neuf, Vingt.

Do you know that the word 'French' in English is Francais in French?

In **PSHE (Personal, Social and Health Education)**, my teacher asked my class to write about our first day in school as homework which you read above. First of all, she is really kind. I think she teaches PSHE and Spanish. I don't do Spanish but my friend Rhiminee does. This subject is about expressing your feelings, knowing that everyone is different with different likes, stick with your opinions, fulfil your ambition and dream you have in life. Be assertive but not aggressive.

> Feed me and I live, yet give me a drink and I die. What am I?

70

Chapter 5: What people think

I asked my friends from my old schools, from church, people who are currently in year 6 and from my new school who are now in year 7 to answer some questions about their experience of moving from year 6 to year 7. I asked them to answer 6 questions. Some were on paper, some by WhatsApp through my mum's phone and some sent their responses by audio.

I got answers from year 7s from different parts of this country and from my cousin in Nigeria. Their answers are very helpful and similar. I also sent questions (through my mum's WhatsApp) to students currently in secondary school, undergraduates, fresh graduates, adults, young parents, elderly parents, grandparents all from different parts of the world from different generations.

A boy called F (can't use his name because I haven't asked for his permission) and me were chosen by the school to talk to an audience of parents and pupils who could start year 7 next year. I was really glad that I was selected to talk to people about my experience. Writing this book really helped me to have a lot of things to say. My speech is also in this book. I was born and ready for that day. So, this is my speech that I used when I went to open evening. Here is what I wrote, printed out and said:

Rebecca Abel's Speech

When I first came to this school, I was a little bit shy when I started. On induction day, everyone just huddled in their own little groups not communicating much as I hung around with my friends from my old school then I realised, I'm really good at talking to people. So, as I began to talk to people, I made new friends. That is one way to make friends. Some people in this school looked like giants and skyscrapers to me because they were so tall and I thought I was tall. But they were not scary because they're normal human beings like me. So, as I explored some places like the library, I thought to myself that there weren't any reasons to be afraid of secondary school. Soon I'll be one of those giant looking people when new year sevens come to the school. But not scary looking.

Many of the teachers were very kind. Some were funny and some strict but in a good way. Since I've made new friends, I've been able to talk to various people. I've settled in very well because I know where all my classes are and I know all the buildings and very few teachers that teach me. My form tutor is very kind and so are the rest of my form group. This school is the right school for you because there are different teachers that can help you with any troubles or feelings you may have. Thank you for listening.

That was what I said twice at the open evening and I had to read it twice in front of 'loads' of adults. I think there were about 85 – 90 people in the hall at each time I stood there reading to them. I was a little terrified about that day because everybody was an adult. Well most of them were. If you have a speech in school that you are going to say, then don't be terrified. I was a bit nervous at the start but what happened was when F said his first, I had confidence in myself. I have a very short recording of my speech but my mum didn't record it in my school because the gadget she was recording my speech with didn't quite work. So, we just had to record my speech at home again. On my YouTube channel, GirlSparkles Abel, I'm going to show the video, it will be called 'My first speech I said in year 7' and I hope you like it.

What I learnt from the opportunity I was given was that I need to look at the audience some times when reading. I was glad that people laughed a bit when I said some funny things. I was also very happy that my family watched me. Some adults and the Headteacher came up to me afterwards to congratulate me about the speech. I felt more confident and happy that I could impress some people.

Any way let me show you the letters that I gave to my friends. Read them and understand what they say. What they say will be very helpful.

> I'm tall when I'm young, I'm short when I'm old. What am I?

Asking students in primary school about their expectations

Questions:

1. What do you expect secondary school to be like?

2. What do you think the children in secondary school will act like?

3. Are you worried about secondary school? Yes/ no (Give reason)

4. Why do you think you need to go to secondary school after primary school?

I expect secondary school to be very scary but fun experience. I think the older children will bully the new children and think they own/rule the school.

Yes I am worried about secondary school because I don't know what to expect. I am also worried for my GCSEs. I hope I can make friends. I need to go to secondary school because I want a good family of my own and I want them to be healthy so I need secondary school to get good education to get a good job to get money.

-Shannon Year 6

I expect secondary school to be hard, scary, brain-burning and very very hard. I think the children in secondary school will greet me and will say "do you want to be friends?"

No. I am not scared about secondary school because I know I will get new friends. I will need spare pencils and pens and a lot of confidence in myself because we still need to work our hardest and keep learning.

-Alfie Year 6

I think secondary school will be very confusing, scary and busy. I also think I will need to write really fast. I think the children in secondary school will act a bit mean and wanting to steal things off us.

Yes I am worried about secondary school because I 'm scared will get lost or not get to my class on time. You need to get to secondary school to get a good job and learn things we still do not know.

-Alexis Year 6

I think secondary school is terrifying because you're the youngest and the others might pick on you. I think the children in secondary school will act all childish and probably pick on me.

Yes I am worried because I don't know my way around and I am nervous about my GCSEs. You need to go to secondary school so you can grow up and get jobs. It is important for your education.

-Kelsey Year 6

I think secondary school is a new chapter of your life. There are bigger opportunities for you. You have more freedom. I feel like when you get to year 7, the year 8s will think we are still too young to be ourselves.

Yes I am quite worried because I'm going to secondary school where not really anyone in my class chose the school I chose. I'm worried if people will stop my learning. I think you need to go to secondary school so you can take bigger challenges. You do your GCSEs so you can get the jobs you want. You meet new people and grow a bigger mind-set.

-Celestina Year 6

I expect secondary school to be fun but also hard. I can not wait to go and I love the idea of secondary school. The children might be kind because they will understand but some people might be angry for different reasons. I am worried because I am sure if everybody will like me. I am not worried because I am excited about everything. I have mixed emotions of secondary school. You need to go to secondary school so that you can learn everything that you will need for life. You can not learn everything in your first years at school.

-Anonymous Year 6

I expect secondary school to be easy and hard sometimes and strict. The secondary school children will be nice, funny, nasty and sensible. No I am not worried about secondary school because I'm going to take no notice of the people that are horrible to me. You need secondary school to learn more work for when you get a job.

-Anonymous Year 6

I expect secondary school to be harder than primary school but different because there will be new sports and new activities to do and learn. I think some will act kind but it depends on their personality. I think they will be able to get along with.

Yes I am worried because the lessons will be too hard and I will not have the time to complete whatever I am doing. I need to got to secondary school so I can learn more and get a good education. So I can make new friends.

-Anonymous Year 6

I expect secondary school to be a lot harder than in year 6 and I think if you don't get it right first time you will get a DT. I think they will act all hard and they will try to start a fight.

I am worried about secondary school because if I don't get my SATs paper correct, I will be put in a low group and then I would get bullied. I think you need to go to secondary school because if you don't, you will not get a job and a good grade.

-Anonymous Year 6

I expect secondary school to be scary, frightening, hard, nice and calm. I think the children in secondary school will be mean but some welcoming.

Yes I am worried because I don't know what the other children will act to me. I need to go to secondary school to get a good education and pass my GCSEs and get a good future.

-Anonymous Year 6

I expect secondary school to be easy and happy once you've been there for at least a term and once you've tried your hardest to achieve your work. I think some of the children will act naughty and like bullies but I also think others will act friendly and kind. I think I won't be scared of secondary because on induction day you'll make new friends and learn lots when you've started your first term. Everyone has to go to secondary school because it is a challenging and higher level of school; you need to go to secondary school so you can do your GCSEs and move onto 6th Form/University.

- Rachel Year 5

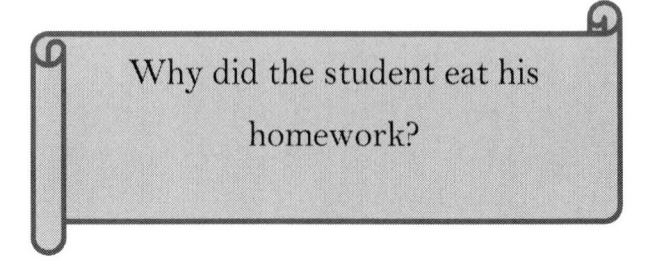

> Why did the student eat his homework?

Asking students who just started year 7 in secondary school

Questions:

1. How did you feel about starting year 7?

2. Do you still have the same feeling about year 7 now? (Yes/no)

3. Did your teachers' information in your primary school help you to prepare for secondary school? (Give reason)

4. Explain why you were happy to start secondary school if not; explain why you were sad to start secondary school?

5. What advice would you give to people who are currently in year 6 and will be moving to year 7 soon?

Well I felt very upset because I was leaving my old school and my friends because they were all going to different secondary schools. I also felt scared. I don't have that feeling anymore because I've got friends who have the same time table as me so we get to go to lessons together.

Yes my teacher's information helped especially in Yr 6, my teacher trained us and talked us through how it would be like: triple the homework, more lessons, different teachers etc.

For me, it was a mixed feeling because all my friends /classmates were at different schools and everyone all had their friends. Also I was scared that I wouldn't get the work therefore I'd get detention.

My advice would be talk to people and make friends. It would make life easier and give confidence. I'm not saying tight bonds if you don't want but it helps a lot to have someone to talk to.

-Rachel Year 7

I felt excited to have more lessons and learn them in more depth but I was upset because I had to leave my old friends behind, also because everything is bigger & different. No I don't have the same feeling anymore because I ended up finding new best friends and when I had been at the school for a couple of days, I became used to it.

Yes my teacher's information helped because in Yr 6 the teachers give you more responsibilities & jobs ready for high school such as: litter picking, truck trolley, school councillor's, learning leading and assembly monitors plus they gave good education. Because in secondary they give you time tables so you know for certain what lessons you have. I also love how you can do so many subjects and study them deeper than you would in primary.

Don't worry, it may seem scary but if you give it a chance it can turn into something beautiful. School wasn't made to occupy kids for 6 hours but to polish your wings so you can fly!

- Rhiminee Year 7

I felt nervous because it's a new school. No I don't have that feeling anymore because I know where to go and I've made a lot of friends.

Yes my teacher's information helped me. They told me to believe in myself and it really helped to make friends. I was happy to start secondary school because it was a new experience. My advice is to believe in themselves and don't be afraid to ask.

Quote: 'Stop trying to fit in when you were born to stand out.

- Nima Year 7

I felt happy because I was starting a new school. Secondary school even better. I have been telling my parents to buy all my stationary and all my uniform before high school started. Yes I still have the same feeling because I've been excited ever since the last term of year Did my teacher's information help me to prepare for secondary school? Kind of because my teacher said you had to carry your bag around with you all the time and when it's a rainy day, take your umbrella or coat to school but bear in mind that you have to carry everything with you.

I was happy and sad to start secondary school. Happy because I've always wanted to be in year 7. Sad because all my friends will be going to different schools. My advice is, don't be afraid. Always try to do your best no matter what has happened. Try not to get detention, be positive, and enjoy all your fun new lessons.

— **Rebecca (me, myself and I) Year 7**

I felt nervous starting secondary school as I knew no one, I also felt like I wouldn't fit in. I don't feel the same because I have 3 friends who are funny, weird and share a lot of things in common with me.

Did my teacher's information in primary school help? No, not really. She didn't talk about secondary school. I was feeling a mixture of these feelings as I was happy to make friends but sad to leave my old friends behind. My advice is to make year 6 last, have fun, don't wish it away because in a blink of an eye you will be in year 7.

— **Callum Year 7**

I felt excited starting secondary school, wasn't very nervous. Yes I still have the same feeling. Did my teacher's information help?

No, my teacher said some daunting things about secondary school! I was happy to start secondary school, I knew I was going to make new friends. My advice is to enjoy yourself because if you don't, it'll reflect on your behaviour.

- Adesola Year 7

In the beginning, it was hard to find my way around the school but after several days I was able to find my way around pretty easily.

No I don't have that feeling anymore. Yes my teacher's information helped because my teachers told me to memorise my timetable in case I lost it. I was excited to start secondary school because there would be new learning and moving around instead of staying in one classroom and getting to know new teachers also making friends with people you've never known before. For my advice, I would say just be yourself and remember your timetable (in case you get lost).

— **Grace Year 7**

I felt very confident and excited to start secondary school. Nope! I don't feel the same way. Did my teacher's information in primary school help? NO. Because most of them never taught in secondary school and therefore have no full idea of what it's like.

I was happy to start secondary school because it is a new environment and has more subjects and lessons. My advice to those in primary school is that you can never be TOO ready to start secondary school no matter what.

-Anonymous Year 7

I felt excited and couldn't even sleep that day before starting school because I was happy to start a new chapter of my life. No I don't have the same feeling because you get to know things you have never known before. But some of the things they teach is kind of what you've learnt in year 6 but in a more complicated way. My teacher's information about secondary school helped a lot because they always told us that when you are in secondary school, things will be different and kind of complicated than primary school and that if you're dull, you have to buckle up and they taught us a lot of moral which is helping me right now. Well I was happy and sad at the same time. I was happy because people will no longer see me as a kid but as a grown up somehow, you know. I was sad because it is hard to leave something you love so much like

I miss my classmates, friends and teachers and it's kind of hard to start in a new and strange environment and it is hard to make friends. I'll advise those in primary school that they shouldn't be scared because before I started secondary school, I felt scared because it was a little hard to start in a new environment and it is kind of strange not being the senior class anymore. But you shouldn't be afraid just go riding and God willingly guide you through all the challenges and difficulties you may be having. Another advice is to always be friendly, avoid bad companies, stick to your studies always be holy and trust me you will make it through secondary school happily.

–Adeola Joy Apata (my cousin) Year 7

I felt anxious and nervous as I was approaching my first day there in secondary school. No I don't have the same feeling anymore. Did my teacher's information in primary school help? Yes, they told me that I shouldn't be nervous because there were many other children who were about to enter their own new schools as well. I was both happy and sad to join high school because I would have to leave some of my close friends from primary school, however, I was happy as well because I could make new friends and meet new people. My advice would be that they shouldn't be afraid of high school even though there is a lot of homework that you have to do and many other things that may seem stressful but you should try your best do your homework at the right time and enjoy your time there.

–Zoe Year 7

I was excited and nervous starting year 7. Yes I still have the same feeling. No my teacher's information did not help me prepare for secondary school because he only told us that we had lots and lots of homework. I was happy to start secondary school because that's another part of an exciting adventure ☺. My advice to those in starting secondary school is to be yourself, trust God and make lots and lots of friends x

–Khadija Year 7

I felt good settling in year 7. Yes I still have the same feeling. Yes my teacher's information in primary school helped because they said you won't feel any different. I'm happy to start secondary school because you have a wide area and you have a good environment. I would advise those in year 6 to never be scared of anyone.

— Joshua Year 7

I felt OK starting secondary school just a bit nervous. No I don't have the same feeling. Yes my teacher's information helped as I knew that I needed to be more organised and try to manage my time. I was happy to start secondary school as I knew some people already going to my high school in my year. My advice is, don't be nervous and don't try to change yourself just because someone tells you to and do homework the day you get it or it will quickly pile up.

— Shewa Year 7

> I am the biggest alphabet as I contain the most water in the world. What am I?

Asking students in year 8 to 11 in secondary school

Questions:

1. How did you feel when you started secondary school? Did you overcome that feeling? How did you overcome that feeling?
2. Do you enjoy secondary school? Why?
3. What advice will you give to students who are starting secondary school?

When I started secondary school, I felt a little bit anxious and I overcame it by thinking it's just a thing you have to go through and it will be over. Do I enjoy secondary school? Yes, kind of. It's exciting because there are loads of new people joining and loads of support and loads of new teachers. To those starting secondary school, I would tell them to find out who are the best staff to talk to if there is a problem. Find out which teachers are good and which aren't. I would tell them which are the best after school clubs to go to.

– Anonymous Year 8

When I started secondary school I was very nervous at first, because I was going into a new school not knowing what to expect and knowing nobody. However as time went on many other people felt the same as me, which I realised so I decided to be confident and was keen to make friends. I talked to as many people as I can, be polite and stay true to myself.

I enjoy secondary school a lot because it gives you more freedom and space to try new things as well as learn new things and gives you a taste of the real world. I say to be confident and don't be scared going into secondary knowing what you want to achieve and then the right friends should follow. Always stay true to you and do what you want to do.

– Anonymous Year 8

When I first started secondary school I wasn't nervous at all because I had been to their open evenings and I was going with friends so I had someone to talk to at all times. I don't enjoy secondary school because there's a lot of pressure to achieve good GCSE. My advice is to focus well in the beginning because it's very hard to catch up when your exams come.

– Anonymous Year 11

I felt nervous at first but as I got to know the people and the students my nerves decreased. Do I enjoy high school? Not really because there is a lot of work to do. My advice is that you should have fun while you can but also balance out your school work because it makes it easier to get through the year.

– Anonymous Year 11

I felt nervous. Yes I overcame it by my parents instilling confidence in me by telling me it will be okay and turned out okay. Do I enjoy secondary school? Sometimes Yes, when I have fun subjects like science, art, cooking and PE. Sometimes No when I have boring subjects like history and geography.

My advice is to try your hardest at everything. Do your homework as early as possible so you will have time for other things. Stay away from bad company and friends. Revise early and hard for exams and take a break. Always go to bed early because it has a big effect on your day (I learnt the hard way!)

– **Anonymous Year 8**

At first it was exciting and fun, meeting new people and just being in a bigger and different environment, then I started to feel overwhelmed by the homework and different subjects and information we had to take in. I overcame this by trying to enjoy the experience and keeping on top of my work and listening to my teacher with a positive mentality of 'I can do It', although I did genuinely enjoy it as I was with the friends I made.

I do enjoy secondary school. It's tough and there are many tests, but ultimately I like learning new things for my general knowledge and being able to contribute to topic conversations with people older than me and I also enjoy understanding things in a more educated manner. However, what really keeps me going is my friends and the fact that so many other girls like me are going through the same situation with tests etc alongside me in my school.

I'd give you the advice to make good, clear notes from year 7, to refer to in next years and also get involved in sports and school activities, make friends with everyone and don't be shy!! Try to always achieve 100% in everything and don't surround yourself with low achievers!!!

– Anonymous Year 10

I felt excited to start grammar school because I always wanted to go there, however I didn't feel nervous or anything as everyone in my class helped each other to find out where to go. I enjoy secondary school because lessons are mostly fun and not boring and that I like going to school because I like to learn new things.

My advice is to try your best to give a good first impression to all the teachers so they don't think that you're one of the 'bad' kids, for example, work hard in class, do some extra work, be proactive, help your classmates when they need help etc.

– Anonymous Year 8

It felt new and different because in secondary school you move around more and have more lessons, I overcame this with time as I got used it. Yes I do enjoy secondary school as you have time to explore subjects and see which one you prefer.

Be open to try new things and have fun but also try hard. Good luck.

– Anonymous Year 10

> Why were the teacher's eyes crossed?

Asking College and University students

Questions:

1. Do you miss your secondary school? (Yes/No) Give reason
2. What would you do differently if you had another chance to go to secondary school?
3. What advice will you give to students who have started secondary?

Yes I miss my secondary school because you get to learn things from very different subjects all at the same time. If I had a second chance, I would spend my free time more wisely! My advice is, work hard towards what you want and not what your friends or social groups want.

— Anonymous (College)

Yes, I miss the learning environment and warm faces that I had grown accustomed to. It was a big change from being taught in school to lectured at the University. If I had a second chance, I would take the time to actually enjoy learning each subject rather than focus on just passing an exam. My advice is to make the most of the learning environment. To use this time to develop your organisation skills and time management skills. It is also never too early to get involved with community volunteering as well as the future.

– Anonymous (Masters level)

Yes I miss my secondary school. What I miss the most are my classmates and teachers especially the teachers that went above and beyond to help us. Nevertheless, after spending about 5 years with them I guess you're bound to miss everyone. If I had another chance I would perhaps learn a musical instrument and read outside my subjects more. My advice is, learn to enjoy every subject. Your mindset about a subject can make a huge impact on how well you do in it.

– **Anonymous (Undergraduate)**

No I don't miss secondary school because I got to meet new people and studied what I really wanted to. If I had a second chance, I will actually do my homework on time and get involved in more things outside of school.

My advice to secondary school starters is to make the most of it. Listen to your teachers and have fun.

– **Anonymous (Fresh graduate)**

I miss the junior years in secondary school because it was more relaxed and there was less pressure. If I have a second chance, I'll do more out-of-school activities

My advice is to be open-minded about everything and everyone. Try lots of different clubs and activities, utilise all of the offers the school has for you and work hard in lessons and with your homework.

- Anonymous (Undergraduate)

No I don't miss my secondary school as I was not there for very long. If I had a second chance, I would probably do more extra-curricular activities within the school or even developing good study habits and less time hanging around in town. My advice is to get on the good side of your teachers it will come a long way as you progress in the later years.

- Anonymous (Fresh graduate)

It was different to primary school because I had to go to different classes for different lessons but as the weeks went on it was easier. Yes I enjoy secondary school because there was loads of things to do and most of all there were different activities that you can partake in after school. I think that when you start year 7 you should be ready to try out different things but also be relaxed and always ask your teacher for help when you need it.

– Anonymous (College)

No, I don't miss my secondary school because I was bullied. If I had a second chance, I would stand up for myself, be more confident and I wouldn't give in to peer pressure like I did.

Always remember who you are no matter the situation. Also it's not the end of the world if you don't have friends.

– Anonymous (Undergraduate)

Yes I miss my secondary school because it was an easy time. If I had a second chance, I would put in more work during GCSE times to get more As. Don't let people get you down, keep your head high and don't let bullies control your life, remember who you are and what you are capable of and take part in all opportunities presented to you.

– Anonymous (Undergraduate)

What do you call a fake noodle?

Asking parents about their experiences in secondary school

Questions:

1. As far as you can remember, what was your experience of starting secondary school?

2. What were your highlights (likes and/or dislikes) about being in secondary school?

3. How did your parents help to prepare you for secondary school?

4. Did you prepare your child(ren) in any way for secondary school? How did you or will you prepare your child for secondary school?

My experience of starting secondary school was exciting but nervous. I liked the variety of subjects and opportunities but disliked the amount of older students (feeling intimidated). My parents prepared me for secondary school through -pep talks, provide with equipment and uniform, help with homework. It was very helpful and encouraging.

– Anonymous (Adult)

Experience – Exciting but also scary because of the fear that I might be punished or asked to do some work for the more senior students (in Nigeria).

Likes- many different teachers, lots of new subjects, new status 'secondary', more independence – walk with friends on the way back home, prep (time after school to complete homework before going home), daily assembly

Dislike- not a lot that I can remember- labour day- when we're given a portion of grass to cut using cutlass.

My parents helped me to prepare for secondary school by supporting me to get ready for entrance examinations, They helped me to select the schools, bought uniform, books and other essentials for school.

I prepared my children for secondary in the UK by researching good schools (based on Ofsted reports, parents' reviews and GCSE results) and ensuring that we lived in the catchment area of the school – early prep. Used past papers online and bought books to get them ready for SAT , attended open evening in their prospective school to have a first hand experience and opportunity to ask questions.

– Anonymous (Finished 31 years ago)

I was very excited when I transitioned into secondary school. I was excited and I looked forward to every single day in secondary school.

I didn't like the fact that I had to read or study everyday not during exams like Primary School.

I had enough tutorials during the holidays ahead of my resumption, they also gave me a lot of prep talk and counselling.

My kids are yet to get to that stage.

– Anonymous (Finished 22 years ago)

I was excited having passed the entrance exam. I like Mathematics a lot but didn't like studying Latin. Now I wish I had put in the effort with this foreign language. Sport was badly resourced hence I lost the chances it could have offered me...

My parents were also excited being the first child to go in my family. They provided me with support within their means...

Although the society and culture were different to mine, there wasn't unbearable problem to get them ready. The infrastructures allowed them to be self motivated. The peer pressures appeared to have also played a part in terms of the essential expenses.

– Anonymous (Adult)

I was happy because I was going to a boarding School and I was scared because I didn't know anyone.

Mine was a new school and had two sets of seniors and we were like a family. I disliked their food but my dad usually brought food for me at the weekend. My dad encouraged me and visited me every weekend so I didn't miss home.

I prepared my children for secondary school by teaching them what they would expect and any subject they don't understand. I make sure I teach them until they understand. I also advised them on what type of friends to make.

– Anonymous (Finished 31 years ago)

My experience of starting secondary school was quite exciting because I already had my older siblings in secondary school and I was looking forward to joining them.

Likes: Going to school with my older siblings; my school uniform(white and white)

Dislikes: Being disciplined by older students; walking a long way to school.

My parents actually tried preparing me by buying school uniform, sandals; school bags, pens and notebooks. I would prepare my child emotionally, physically and psychologically.

– Anonymous (Adult)

I was excited to be leaving home for the 1st time. Boarding house seemed like little heaven – away from my mum's control.

Seniority – older students had the authority to send junior ones on errands and punish them. I loved school better when I became a senior. My parents helped by buying things I needed for boarding house – school uniforms, toiletries and provisions. I am supporting my son to prepare for his exams to get him into a selective secondary school. His siblings are still in primary school.

– Anonymous (Adult)

Well, at the time I started secondary school in 1986, my parents were separated, myself and my siblings were with my dad....He was a busy man....though he encouraged me(the children) to value formal education, the nature of his work then, did not give him much time to follow up on our academic performance... So there you have it, I had to wade through secondary school myself.

My secondary school days were full of both happy and unpleasant memories. I remember I disliked being flogged along with others for noise making but I cannot forget the wonderful moments with other students on Fridays, as we assemble to worship GOD..I also remember my English language teacher, she was a sweet teacher, a good motivator...

Like earlier stated, I had to do everything myself... Even when it's time to pay school bill, I'll collect the fees from my Dad... Pay into the school account myself... Represent myself and my siblings at the parents/teachers conference....

Well, today, by God's grace, as a parent I collaborate with my hubby, we talk about virtually everything that concerns the children with them, including preparation for secondary school education. We drop them at school and pick them on time.... They follow us to do necessary payments, purchase or shopping for school materials.... We also have family study time together. The children are assured of us making time out of no time to attend their PTA Parents/Teachers Conferences.

– Anonymous (Finished 25 years ago)

Very scary but enjoyed shopping for my new uniform. Loved all the different subjects like cooking and woodwork and experiments in science.

Didn't like the size of school and some horrible children. My parents did not really prepare or encourage me. I tried to prepare mine by helping them with homework and encourage them to study but don't remember preparing them in other ways think I could have done more.

– Anonymous (Adult)

I remember when I was about to start my secondary school. I had mixed feelings because I was going to be in a boarding school without my family members. One thing I will never forget was my mum taught me how to take care of myself. I knew how to prepare myself for school. My dislike in secondary school was that seniors always send juniors on errands and if you were to find yourself in a senior block as a junior student, you will run errands through out the day. Sometimes the food served were not nice especially the beans. It was very watery and tasteless. I liked that it made me to be more independent and also to know how to prioritise things. I also liked the fact that I can survive in any environment I find myself in.

– Anonymous (Adult)

It was a mixture of experiences: Friendships that does not go beyond school gates, fear of the teacher's cane, school mothers, textbooks. My highlights are teachers' cane, friendship. Did my parents prepare me for secondary school? I cannot remember that happening, they just provide what you need. Did I prepare my children? Yep. We talked about being organised to enable them stay on top of workload, staying safe on the road, friendship group and using wisdom, practice run with travel, waking up.

– Anonymous (Adult)

I was a little anxious and often confused. I liked the space and facilities. I enjoyed the academic challenge. I disliked always getting into fights with bullies. Dad taught me how to take care of myself and would talk about science with me. Mum bought me books, talked about politics and religion with me encouraged me to study.

My child is not old enough for school yet, but yes I will prepare him. I will prepare him academically by teaching him science and maths. I'll teach him to be an independent learner i.e. to study independently. I will help him take up team sports. I'll teach him to be confident and sociable by taking him to clubs such as scouts etc. I'll teach him how to deal with bullies.

– Anonymous (Adult)

I was excited. I couldn't wait to leave primary school so that people will start seeing me as a big girl but soon after I started I realised I was in the lowest class and people still saw me as a small girl ☺

Likes- it was a mixed school (boys and girls), school uniform

Dislikes- having to run away or hide from seniors to avoid errands and bullying, the very strict regimented life...there was time for everything: wake up time, bathing time, prep time, etc, having to queue for food, fetching of water, ironing, etc

My dad took me round the school before I resumed. I was taught to always to the right thing, so never got into trouble in school and I didn't allow any negative peer influence.

I plan to instil godly character into my children that they would always do the right thing and shine as light wherever they find themselves.

– Anonymous (Adult)

I was posted to the secondary school I attended by the Local Government Authority from the primary school I attended.

I asked a friend in my neighbourhood who was a student of my new school to take me to the school, since I didn't know the place, and he did. I took my mother to the school for her to know my new school, and my parents made provision for me to begin.

MY LIKES AND DISLIKES.

(a) It was a school for all comers with no discrimination of social status or class

(b) It was a bit distant from home, thus enabling me to learn to make some distal movement away from home unaided

(c) I learned simple physical labour activities such as bush cleaning in school, since the school compound was very large, requiring us the students to cut grass and do other menial activities.

(d) Learning aids (such as textbooks) were provided by the government

DISLIKE
Corporal punishment was common in public schools in those days.

HOW MY PARENTS HELPED TO PREPARE ME FOR SECONDARY SCHOOL
The only thing I remember is that they got me school kits (uniform, sandals, etc) and books

DID I PREPARE MY CHILD IN ANY WAY FOR SECONDARY SCHOOL..., HOW?
(a) I helped my child with counselling sessions to prepare him emotionally and psychologically.

(b) I trained him on crossing the major roads to and from schools. This was a major challenge for him, having to go and return unaided, and most drivers on Nigerian roads are unqualified to drive. (He never went out unaided until this time)

(c) I encourage him to act independently and we both keep an enabling atmosphere for him to express himself and be guided as regards whatever experience he has.

– Anonymous (Finished 28 years ago)

It was an experience of excitement that I would be learning unfamiliar subjects like Latin and Mathematics. What I liked about Secondary school include making new friends, the discipline of following a daily routine of waking up early in the morning to prepare for school and creating time after school hours for homework to be submitted to the class teacher the following day. Extracurricular activities including Inter-house sports and Inter-school debate competitions would ever be remembered for good. The distasteful side of secondary school life was the bullying by the seniors. Parental help in preparing for secondary school in the rural area where I had my elementary school education was zero because there were no after-school lessons or coaching outfits during that time. All my children grew up in an urban environment and they had the privilege of attending private schools where their teachers organised after-school tutorials for them. Occasional checking of their class work was also helpful.

– Anonymous (Finished 56 years ago)

For me transiting from primary to secondary school was initially exciting because my other friends/classmates were already in secondary but getting into the boarding house wasn't easy for me because I was always missing home, no mummy, daddy and aunties to take care of me, I had to take care of myself and my things.

My likes was the fact that I could eat my provisions the way I liked, my dislikes was that we had to wake up very early, fetch water and the worst was seniors' constant punishments.

They helped my providing all I needed, handed me over to a teacher and ensuring that my elder sister tried her best to take care of me.

Well I look forward to preparing my daughter in the nearest future.

– Anonymous (Adult)

My experience of starting secondary school was filled with joy, as I had then thought going to a boarding secondary school was joining the league of big boys. Also, some of my primary school mates and lesson mates were all there. So I wasn't a fish out of water.

My likes then was being in companies of my childhood friends, making new friends, living free without my parents, schooling was an adventure.

Dislike then where senior bullying, early morning drills, poor sanitary conditions etc

As I was quite young then, I didn't know what preparations my parents did. All I know was items required by the school authorities were provided for me by my parents as it was a fad during my time to send your children to boarding school. So, when I got to that stage, my parents announced to those who cared to ask, which secondary school I would attend.

My son will not be due to join the secondary school band wagon in another 2years, as I want him to be better prepared for secondary school.

I intend to prepare him by letting him understand how important this stage in his life is. How his future is dependent on his secondary schooling. How he needs to develop himself by reading more, further explore his passion and understanding his body better etc.

– Anonymous (Adult)

I was excited going to a boarding school and I already had my immediate elder sister in the same school. I didn't like the house work that I had to do like cutting grass and washing plates. I loved the new friends that I made who had different cultural views.

My Parents always wanted their children to be independent and by sending us to a boarding school helped us to achieve this. We were able to take good decisions and also develop our leadership abilities.

I will always want my children to learn how to be independent too and also learn in a multi-cultural environment.

– Anonymous (Adult)

I finished secondary school almost 60 years ago and I still remember my very first day. I was happy to go because it was a boarding school on the capital of the old Western Region of Nigeria.

It was an opportunity to leave my small town (which incidentally was the headquarters of the old Ondo Province of Nigeria).

– Anonymous (Finished 60 years ago)

I was in secondary school form one in 1965 which is 52 years ago. My experience of starting secondary school was quite exciting. It was a boarding school about 60 miles from where I lived. Traveling to start school was interesting. I made a lot of friends.

I liked our teachers because they gave us solid background in education and taught us very well. I also enjoyed the company of my classmates. Some of the senior girls were very bossy. There were many rules and regulations to follow. These rules and regulations however helped to mould our characters and made us become responsible adults.

I was brought up by my uncle and his wife who prepared me adequately and ensured that I passed the entrance exam and taught me how to look after myself in the boarding school. Yes, I prepared my children for secondary school both in terms of academics and how to cope psychologically with secondary school life.

– Anonymous (Finished 52 years ago)

I was excited to start secondary school, a bigger school and different people to meet. It also helped that my older sister was there so I was confident that I'll be safe and happy. I was ready to leave primary school.

I liked most of my classes (math, English, Spanish and French). Most of the classes they offered seemed quite silly to me, they didn't strengthen my areas of strength and thought they were a waste of time. The teachers were fine, not challenging and not terrifying. Didn't really have any role models there.

I didn't like the social aspect of secondary school, it was very segregating and it was difficult to find my place among groups of people in the first few weeks.

My parents didn't really prepare me for secondary school. I had older siblings so they helped some of the time before going.

Currently, I don't have children but if I did, I would like to think that I'll have a more active role in their preparation as well as their time at school. It is a life changing period so parents should be invested in that time.

– Anonymous (Adult)

I finished secondary school 21 years ago and definitely had the excitement of being in a new environment and meeting new people.

My likes were freedom to go to school and come back on my own without school bus and less supervision, freedom of spending my upkeep money as I wish and my dislikes were d constant punishment and flogging from teachers and senior students when you get into their trouble.

My parents helped me by advising me to do well in my studies so I can excel in life. Yes I prepared my child well for secondary school by making sure she entered the school at the right age i.e finishing her primary education in primary 6 before writing common entrance exams and I also prepared her emotionally & spiritually by advising her not to mingle with the wrong friends.

– **Anonymous (Finished 21 years ago)**

My experience was very daunting as I was quite a small individual so I felt like I would get lost in the crowd of big people. My likes about secondary school were the times when I could play football and show my athletic ability at different competitions, my dislikes were the ridicule I sometimes got from peers around me. They brought me extra reading and school equipment essential for my development.

– **Anonymous (Young adult)**

Starting secondary school for me was a daunting experience because it was an all-girls boarding school and I had never been away from my family prior to that time. I played along with the excitement that I was going to a prestigious school (which was as if I was going to Oxford or Cambridge or Harvard). Everyone was excited for me because I passed the exams but I had mixed feelings.

The reality dawned on me when we travelled about 4 hours by car to a remote place with huge buildings, total strangers and tall ladies who were like big Aunties back then. My parents arranged my bed and cupboard, picked a 'school mother' for me and gave me sufficient money to last me for a few months at least before the next visiting day. I wept that night and felt lonely after my family left even though everyone was trying to be friendly.

After a few days, I got used to the routine of washing clothes, fetching water, morning bells, Saturday house inspections, morning duty, improvising wisely (like sewing torn clothes), study time, meal times, timetables, activities and generally taking control of my life by myself. It then began to make sense that I wasn't the only new girl on the block.

Secondary school was a big formative year for me. I made good choices that I built on and a few bad choices I learnt from. Being in a girls-only school, it was a great time of bonding with friends whom I still remember till today, breaking up and making up friendship ties, working in a team to get homework done without parents' assistance. My proper faith journey started in secondary school with a love for Chapel activities, getting involved and feeling at home away from home. I had to grow up quickly even though I learnt most things at home but this time, more independently. In a boarding school, you learn to monitor your progress yourself but your parents see the result at the end of term.

In my days, there wasn't a lot of technology around to distract our learning and we learnt to stick together to achieve a common goal. My confidence was built and I can look back now and be more appreciative of steps taken by my parents to give me the best education and to lay a very firm foundation for the future for me. So, my advice to pupils moving from primary to secondary school is to enjoy every moment of secondary school days.

Apart from supplying all the necessary items required for school, I will prepare my children by equipping them with every valuable information available out there, starting off a discussion at the right time, developing their confidence further and teaching them skills to aid their independence. I will encourage them to make it a formative time where they learn all they can and explore in the right direction because their today has a big role to play in their tomorrow.

– Anonymous (Finished over 30 years ago)

>Person 1: Knock knock
>Person 2: Who's there?
>Person 1: Dewey
>Person 2: Dewey who?
>Person1: Dewey really have homework on the first day of school?

Chapter 6: Summary of my project

This project has helped me to realise that no matter who you are either white or black, short or tall, girl or boy, young or old, with or without parents, the experiences are almost the same but in different ways.

From the year five and sixes, I saw that they are scared of secondary school and their GCSEs. Most of them are scared of secondary because of the older children and getting lost in the *big* school. I had the exact feeling when I was in year five and six; since secondary school is much bigger than primary school you would think that you will get lost easily but actually, once you get used to the school, you will know everywhere as quickly as a flash. Rachel - who is the only year five – is worried about GCSEs. What???!!! Even I am not thinking of that yet! My advice to her is that she shouldn't be worried yet because she still has over a year to calm everything down by getting her 11+ exams and SATs done before secondary school.

From the year sevens' perspectives, I would say that at first they were a bit scared when they entered (since they were in a different environment), they overcame their worriedness by communicating with other students in their year. Now I have many friends than I did in my primary school and most of them are from completely different schools. From the year 8 – 11's perspective, I would say that the years 8's were okay with the flow of secondary school because one of them said that they were not scared at all. If you go to most of the open evenings, you might not be afraid of the secondary school environment anymore. One thing I also spotted was about balancing your homework. Basically, once you have learnt something important, you should jot it down in a notebook (not a piece of paper because it might get lost). You may not love all your subjects except you are incredibly keen on learning. I love most of my subjects but I find geography and history boring the most. I'm hoping it'll get better though. Surprisingly, geography and history are some people's favourite subjects like my Grandpa. From the adults' perspective, they all liked their secondary schools and many of them still remember their first day after many years. Even my mum still sings some of her secondary school songs! Lol!

Nerves

Almost everybody talked about being nervous or anxious or having mixed feelings when they were starting high school. It shows that we all have some feelings attached to any change we are going through in life. The only difference between what makes it a happy ending or unhappy ending is how we deal with it. People deal with these feelings in different ways. Some people withdraw and wait for someone to talk to them because they want to experience new friendship and company; some people are very quiet watching how others deal with the new environment so they can do the same and settle in properly. Some people only stick around their old friends because they may not have good communicating skills; some people start a conversation with someone new like I did and that is a way to start making friends.

Friends

Most people are friendly and with so many friends but some are not good at making friends (but it doesn't mean they are unfriendly). Friends can either be a good crowd to be around or the opposite. Many parents warn their children of mixing with the wrong crowd. You don't have to force yourself to make thousands of friends. Make yourself friendly and be nice to everyone even if they are different from you. Some people will try to be nasty sometimes but it could be that they are having a bad day so ignore them and keep smiling. My mum says "don't let other people's mood dictate your mood" but be in charge of your behaviour. The other years don't often want to be friends with year 7s because they feel that we are little children. In my school, they have this 'buddy' system where older children from the other years help you to gain confidence in year 7. That system was very comforting ; I soon one day want to be a 'buddy'. Just like someone said that it's not the end of the world if you don't have friends.

Different types of secondary school

There are different kinds of secondary or high schools. Some students go to a boarding school, or day school, or selective school, or non-selective school or Independent school or home school or religious school etc. Some schools wear uniforms while others allow students to wear whatever they like. That's non-uniform every day? Can't imagine what that would be like.

Around the world, it seems it is common for primary school children to write exams to get a good secondary school. Hmm.. I might be wrong. Whichever school you end up going to, making the best out of what you have is very important to get you to where you want to be. Some parents have checked the report of the school their children will be going to, they have spoken to other parents who have children in the school and some parents don't bother about things like that. I think it is very important for a child to have a say in the school also because it's not the parents who will go to the school to face different teachers and friends and adjust in the new environment. It is better to involve the child in making the decision too so that parents, guardians and children can work together just as my parents did with me.

More effort

The higher you go in class the more challenging it will be (I don't want to use the word difficult). Some of those in the colleges and universities said that if they had a second chance, they'll like to put in more effort into exams, not piling up homework etc. In high school, students are not only awarded on their academic performance because some are really trying hard but still not getting it. Students are also given scores on good effort. It is normal for some people to like or not like some subjects because of the teacher but it is wiser if you don't allow a teacher's mood or other things to stop you from liking a subject. You could ask other adults for help or check online for solutions. My mum showed me how to use *bitesize* to revise any topic and use YouTube to find tutorials. You just need to put in a lot of effort because it is your future we are talking about and not your friend or teacher's future.

Getting involved in activities

Opening up your mind to learn something new is very important. Some have said they would have loved to learn another language or learn to play an instrument or get more involved in some school clubs. You never know if you like something until you have tried it yourself because other people may have a different opinion about some activities in school. If you don't try different activities, you may miss that opportunity for the rest of your life and then feel guilty or you have to pay a lot of money to learn it when you finish secondary school- as my mum says. In addition, it is possible that you may not have the time to learn it anymore so it would be nice to have a chance to be sporty or speak a different language fluently. If you get a chance to be in a sports team, that could be your most memorable moment.

Homework

Right from primary school, the one thing almost everyone talks about is the volume of homework you will get in high school. This is reality and non-fiction!!! Homework piles up easily if you don't do them on time. In secondary school, you are expected to grow up on time by organising yourself and being more responsible. If you forget to do your homework, sometimes teachers give a second chance and then it goes on to a detention.

Freedom/independence

Students have more freedom in secondary schools because you are allowed to walk home yourself, you have pocket money to spend as you wish and you get to make more friends. You might have a whole day to yourself with no brothers or sisters disturbing you, which is calming especially for me.

Age

Students start secondary school at different ages in different parts of the world. I think every child should be given the right to education and they need to be mature enough to handle the challenges they might face. I was told that if I was in a different country, I could have started secondary school earlier or later. In the UK, the official age for starting is at 11+ years old. In most parts of the USA, junior high is for those aged 12 to 14 and senior high for students aged 15 to 17. In Australia, it is 12 years. Some start as early as 9 years old in Nigeria? Do you know that by law, all children under the age of 16 *must* attend school? They call it compulsory education 👍

Bullying-seniority

My idea of a boarding school in my generation is terrifying especially from films/books. I read about bullying in some of the Jacqueline Wilson books that I have read like *'Bad girls'* where a girl was being bullied but her older friend saved her; *'Cliff Hanger'* where this boy is being bullied by this girl but in the end they have a wonderful relationship. *'Vicky Angel'* was where a girl's best friend died and she started being mean to people but people were nice back to her; *'Cookie'* was about this girl who experienced bullying both at home and school. Her dad was not very nice to her nor her mum because he got angry so easily, at school, this girl named Sky bullied and teased her of her size. Her mum was very slim but her dad was broad so she took after her dad not liking that idea. *'Sleepover'* was another book from Jacqueline Wilson, it talked about a girl who was new to a school, and she joined a group of best friends who also wanted to be her best friend. Chloe was part of this group. Daisy was the name of the new girl. She invited her best friends round for a birthday party at her house and Chloe teased Daisy because she had an older sister with disability. Another mean thing that Chloe did was giving Daisy a DVD for a birthday present. The front cover said 'One Dalmatians' but the film inside the DVD case was a horror film and Chloe knows that she is scared easily. When Chloe was scared one day, Daisy wasn't mean back, she helped her...

But, hey! Secondary school is the coolest place to be in some generations. Two wrongs don't make a right nor two rights make a wrong. If you help a bully to do the right things, you never know if they could be your best friend in the whole world. In boarding schools, some of the younger students are usually picked on by the older students. In my secondary school, most people just mind their own business but I have seen a fight about to start but no one actually fought; I also heard about a fight from my friend but yeah you'll be fine. Don't worry because my hope for you is that you will never get bullied or get into a fight. Different names were used to describe bullying like seniority. Bullying can affect students in different ways. It makes some sad, it makes some aggressive by fighting back and it makes some pressured into joining a gang where others could protect them. Bullying is common but you can have someone (like a teacher or an adult) to talk to about it. I think parents should be more friendly with their children so they can tell you if they are having problems in school or not. Parents are supposed to know their children better than anyone else does and they will know if their children are struggling in school or not. Sometimes it is helpful when children have other adults in their lives that they can talk to if their parents are not there for them.

Corporal punishment

In the older generation, teachers used to whip or hit students with cane and give them other types of hard punishment. Phew!!! I'm so glad I was not born in that generation! By the way, when adults say 'flog', they mean whip or hit - just learnt that ☺. In *my* generation, my school uses the C1 – first warning, C2 – second warning and C3 – remove from the class to do work with senior staff. Detentions are also given to students who are late or disrupting learning in class. The new behaviour system is helping the classroom to be a better place to learn because people like me who *want* to learn, have a better potential of doing well in a calm learning environment. As I said earlier, the troublemakers are out of the classroom in a blink of an eye. I have a longer and detailed lesson now that I have peace in the classroom.

Physical provision

Almost everyone from different generations said that their parents/guardians provided them with all of their needs (uniform, school shoes, books, stationery, school bag etc). Some parents expect their children to figure out what they need to do by themselves. Some parents go further by discussing with their children about the big change. It is very helpful for parents to find time to discuss with their children even if it's telling stories about their own experience in school and how they solved some problems, it will help the child. Then they will know that other people have faced the same thing they will face or are facing. My parents told me about their different experiences and even though it was in a different environment and different century (just to make it sound like a very long time ago ☺), I gained some lessons from the talk. I got more confident and I knew a bit of what to expect. My mum's experience of teaching briefly in a secondary school also helped me to prepare emotionally and psychologically for the big responsibility of being in high school.

Preparation:

Students need to prepare physically and mentally for high school because you will be meeting with different kinds of people from different homes, different backgrounds with different opinions. You may not like some people's attitude and they may not like you either. Therefore, if you're not prepared to deal with these differences, you may always be in a mood. Also because of the work you are given in secondary school, you could feel under pressure sometimes but planning your time will really help. Don't wait till the end of your deadline before submitting your homework. Try to do it immediately instead of playing games or watching TV. That's self control! Not easy right? ☺

Checklist

☐ Did you register for the selective school exams popularly known as '11+ exams' in year 5? There's no harm in trying.

☐ Have you attended different open evenings of different schools? Have an open mind and ask questions.

☐ Have you thought about the distance and travel plan to and from school?

☐ Have you bought your equipment (stationery and uniforms)? Remind your parents/Guardians nicely.

☐ Do you know the activities available in the school you want to go to? Sports clubs, breakfast clubs, afterschool clubs.

☐ Have you thought of learning an instrument or a different language? At least try it so you can decide better and not regret when you're older. In my school, there were try outs for instruments. ☺Why not give it a try? ☺

☐	Do you have a personal time table to organise yourself at home better? Bedtime, study time, homework time, playtime etc.

☐	Do you have a notebook for jotting down what you need to remember? This helped me to remember some of the points I have written in this book.

☐	Have you watched my book reviews on YouTube- GirlSparkles Abel?

> Knock, knock —Who's there?- Ashe—Ashe who? Bless you!
>
> Knock, knock —Who's there?- lettuce- Lettuce who? Lettuce in and you'll find out!
>
> Knock, knock —Who's there?- leaf – Leaf who? Leaf me alone!

Appendices

Please could you help me make a decision on the title and charity to choose? Your comments will be really helpful.

Suggested titles (Add your own)

- ☐ My transition process @ 11: From primary to secondary school
- ☐ A non-fiction process - Transitioning from primary to secondary school
- ☐ School is Epic!!!: From SAT to GCSE
- ☐ School is Epic!!!: Transitioning from primary to secondary school
- ☐ Rebecca @ 11 says "School is epic!" - Transitioning from primary to secondary
- ☐ I can't do it...yet ! – Transitioning from primary to secondary school
- ☐ Primary to secondary – my transitioning process @11 years old
- ☐ Je m'appelle Rebecca - Transitioning from primary to secondary school

- ☐ _____

Suggested charities (Add your own)

- ✓ Youngstars club
- ☐ YMCA
- ☐ CodeClub
- ☐ George Eliot Hospital Children's centre
- ☐ My Secondary school
- ☐ My primary school

- ☐ _____

Comments/Questions

_____

_____

If you have any questions, write them down or ask in question time.

Thank you very much.

Rebecca Abel   *Rebecc@*

Please fill this page if you are in primary school.

Questions:

1. What do you expect secondary school to be like?

_____
_____

2. What do you think the children in secondary school will act like?

_____
_____

3. Are you worried about secondary school? Yes/ no (Give reason)

_____
_____

4. Why do you think you need to go to secondary school after primary school?

_____
_____

Please fill this page if you have just started year 7 in secondary school.

Questions:

1. How did you feel about starting year 7?

2. Do you still have the same feeling about year 7 now? (Yes/no)

3. Did your teachers' information in your primary school help you to prepare for secondary school? (Give reason)

4. Explain why you were happy to start secondary school if not; explain why you were sad to start secondary school?

5. What advice would you give to people who are currently in year 6 and will be moving to year 7 soon?

Please fill this page if you are in year 8 to 11 in secondary school

Questions:

1. How did you feel when you started secondary school? Did you overcome that feeling? How did you overcome that feeling?

   _____
   _____
   _____

2. Do you enjoy secondary school? Why?

   _____
   _____
   _____

3. What advice will you give to students who are starting secondary school?

   _____
   _____
   _____

Please fill this page if you are in College and University.

Questions:

1. Do you miss your secondary school? (Yes/No) Give reason

___

2. What would you do differently if you had another chance to go to secondary school?

___

3. What advice will you give to students who have started secondary?

___

Please fill this page if you are a parent/guardian.

Questions:

1. As far as you can remember, what was your experience of starting secondary school?

_____

_____

_____

2. What were your highlights (likes and/or dislikes) about being in secondary school?

_____

_____

_____

3. How did your parents help to prepare you for secondary school?

_____

_____

_____

_____

4. Did you prepare your child(ren) in any way for secondary school? How did you or will you prepare your child for secondary school?

_____

_____

_____

_____

Fundraising (https://www.gofundme/RebeccaAbel)

Hi! My name is Rebecca and I am 11 years old. I am writing a book on my transition process from Year 6 to Year 7 and I have spent so much time writing this book. The reason I am writing this book is to help pupils who are nervous, unsettled or having mixed feelings about moving into secondary/high school to be more confident, aim to be the best and give them some important information they may not get from anyone else.

It's time for me to publish it but I need your kind support to raise funds. I have just one page left to complete and that is my Thank You page. I want to add you to my book as one of those who helped me fulfil my dream of being an author. Please support me as I am donating to two charities: Youngstars club (30%), My Primary and Secondary schools (30%). The remaining 40% is for publishing my book. Thank you.

#SchoolIsEpic

```
H R T R A H G H F L Z X Y D N H Q P N K
I M B J W W H Y T S O Y G R U U Y O B P
Z K W D Q V V Y K B S B I X O P I S F H
M G M H G S W T J Y Q F U O M T B K T S
E U E H E G H J U C G M W Z L S S C V I
R W S O B M Y J V U J E H S D V I I M N
D J Z I G D V S X P A T E E R B D B H A
K X C R C R I I O N S K H I A D A U Y P
Z Q X A R W A F E C A C R D M T B J U S
E C N E I C S P I B N I C U A H T X U L
V I Y V K Q W T H E N Y F T V X I Y K F
K S E X W F A N R Y T C R S W M O I L B
U H P P Z M B F Q B J C I S C C I P I M
M X S Y E M O X R P S U N S V C R X T Z
C H O H S O G E R M A N D E B S L U E A
E J T H D Y O Z A H C P O N V J M E R N
Z A Z T V I N T R O Q B Y I I Q L B A I
M Y E S V V K V D X E Q U S D H E M C C
L C W C O M P U T I N G G U P V K Y Y V
H J H D Z E M D V H C I A B Q X W Z C I
```

ART
BUSINESSSTUDIES
COMPUTING
DRAMA
FOODTECH
FRENCH
GEOGRAPHY
GERMAN
HISTORY
LITERACY
MATHEMATICS
MUSIC
PSHE
SCIENCE
SPANISH

Feedback – tell me what you have learnt

Many readers may have questions. If you go onto my YouTube channel (GirlSparkles Abel) for my book reviews, you can write your questions in the comment box. Now is your chance to express what you have in your mind. Write down your comments and questions. What bits do you not understand about this book? What has encouraged you? What could I do to improve this book?

_____

_____

_____

Questions for the author:

_____

_____

_____

Answers:

> Page 27 – 1) Bungalows don't have stairs   2) Current President of the USA   3) You just said it
> Page 42 – Reflection
> Page 51 – History
> Page 70 – Fire
> Page 75 – Candle or Pencil
> Page 82 – Because the teacher said it was a piece of cake
> Page 95 – Alphabet 'C'
> Page 102 – Because she couldn't control her pupils
> Page 108 - Impasta

Solution

```
+ + T R A + + + + + + Y + + + + + +
+ + + + + + + + + + + R + + + + + +
+ + + + + + + + + + + + O + + + + H
M G + + + + + + + + + + + T + + + S
+ U E + + + + + + + + + + + S + + I
+ + S O + + + + + + + S D + + I + N
+ + + I G + + + + + + + E R + + H A
+ + + + C R + + + S + H I A + + + P
+ + + + + A + + C + C + D M + + + S
E C N E I C S P I + N + + U A + + + +
+ + + + + + + T H E + + + T + + + + +
+ + + + + A + R Y + + + S + + + + L +
+ + + P + M + F + + + + S + + + + I +
+ + S + E + O + + + + + S + + + + T +
+ H + H + O G E R M A N + E + + + E +
E + T + D + + + + + + + N + + + R +
+ A + T + + + + + + + + I + + + A +
M + E + + + + + + + + + S + + + C +
+ C + C O M P U T I N G + U + + + Y +
H + + + + + + + + + + B + + + + +
```

```
         (Over,Down,Direction)
               ART(5,1,W)
        BUSINESSSTUDIES(14,20,N)
            COMPUTING(4,19,E)
              DRAMA(15,6,S)
             FOODTECH(8,13,SW)
              FRENCH(8,13,NE)
            GEOGRAPHY(2,4,SE)
              GERMAN(7,15,E)
             HISTORY(19,7,NW)
             LITERACY(19,12,S)
           MATHEMATICS(1,18,NE)
               MUSIC(1,4,SE)
               PSHE(4,13,SW)
             SCIENCE(7,10,W)
              SPANISH(20,9,N)
```

Printed in Great Britain
by Amazon